SELECTED LEGAL ISSUES IN

CATHOLIC SCHOOLS

SR. MARY ANGELA
SHAUGHNESSY,
SCN, J.D., PH.D.

THE SECONDARY SCHOOLS
DEPARTMENT NATIONAL CATHOLIC
EDUCATIONAL ASSOCIATION

Second Printing 2013
ISBN No.   1-55833-422-X
Part No.   LEG-22-1416

TABLE OF CONTENTS

ACKNOWLEDGEMENTS

I WISH TO THANK SISTER MARY FRANCES TAYMANS, SND, PH.D., Executive Director of NCEA's Secondary Department, for her support and encouragement of all my work, and especially this text.

I am grateful to two dear friends: Father Michael Huggins, Associate Professor of Nursing at Bellarmine University in Louisville, Kentucky, who patiently explains to me medical concepts, canonical issues and offers me a priest's view of many issues; and Dr. Karen Juliano, president of Notre Dame Academy in Tyngsboro, Massachusetts. In 1978, still in our twenties, I became principal and she vice-principal of Nazareth Academy in Wakefield, Massachusetts. We learned administration by trial and error. Today, as a seasoned administrator, Karen is always ready to let me bounce ideas off her and ask her how she would handle thorny situations.

I am also grateful to my religious community, the Sisters of Charity of Nazareth, and its leadership for giving me the opportunities and education to minister in Catholic education. I am grateful to members of my family who keep me grounded and sane in moments when the process of speaking, consulting and writing seems to overcome me.

Lastly, I thank all of you who may read this text. I pray that it may help make the law a more Gospel-based reality and a practical compass for your day-to-day work with young people. May God bless you.

Mary Angela Shaughnessy, SCN, J.D., Ph.D.
August 2008

DEDICATION

WITH LOVE AND PRIDE, I dedicate this text to my sister, Janet Shaughnessy Kellogg. If a person is very blessed, she may have a sister who is more than a blood relative, a sister who gives far beyond what anyone could reasonably expect, a sister who is a second mother to nieces and nephews, and a friend of the heart. My sister, Janet, is all these and more. Janet is a loving wife and a very busy advertising executive, yet she always finds the time to be involved in our nieces and nephews' lives and now, the next generation. She never misses a play, a game, an awards ceremony or a competition. She works at the school fundraisers. She is a true Catholic educator; where else does a child see the faith lived out if not in the family?

In the midst of her many responsibilities, Janet is always there for me. She has typed manuscripts (sometimes with very little notice), transcribed tapes, and done many things I would have no right to expect her to do. She has many talents and she shares them all.

Since the deaths of our parents, Janet holds the family together. She gathers everyone for celebrations and has assumed the role of family archivist and record keeper. She is an excellent cook and baker; she ensures that our mother's recipes are faithfully followed and carefully recorded for the next generation.

I am blessed to have a sister who is also my friend.

INTRODUCTION

THE FIRST EDITION OF THIS BOOK appeared over fifteen years ago. Since then much has happened in the Catholic educational world. No one could have foreseen the school shootings, the sexual abuse crisis in the church, the scandals and convictions of administrators and teachers, the rising occurrence of violence among our students, and so many other events. Readers who were in education fifteen years ago or more know that we now live in a different world than we did then. While computers were part of the earlier world, they were very expensive and many schools had few, if any, available to students. The Internet came into being and suddenly, students could "surf" the net and arrive at unsafe places and meet unsavory persons on line. All the while, parents and society seem to demand more from educators: to keep young people safe while teaching them values, morality and the Catholic faith.

This text is modeled on the first edition, but it is updated and contains new topic chapters and discussion/reflection questions. Administrators may wish to use the readings and questions as part of a professional development program. It is my hope that this text will provide both information and a process for shared reflection. Each chapter presents information concerning legal issues related to the topic area and is followed by questions for discussion.

Note: *Some of the chapters contain content that first appeared in articles written by the author for the NCEA NOTES newsletter. Cases are referenced for illustrative purposes, as examples of legal issues that face Catholic educators. Complete citations can be found in the Works Cited page, which is not intended to be comprehensive.*

Chapter One

ETHICS AND THE LAW: IS THERE A RELATIONSHIP?

THE LAST TWENTY YEARS have found many Catholic educators and ministers facing legal issues in ways not previously imagined. There are no indications that the situation is improving. Many teachers and administrators express exhaustion and exasperation at the plethora of seemingly new issues, new laws and new regulations that emerge on a regular basis. Some educators still cling to an unrealistic hope that the times will change, litigation and threatened litigation will subside and lawmakers will turn their attention from education to another issue. Hoping for a return to the "good old days" is not a very effective approach to dealing with today's legal issues. It is better to know the issues and the laws affecting those issues than it is to guess at them when confronting the situation.

When encountering a situation with legal ramifications, persons often ask, "Can I do this legally?" An administrator may ask, "Can I legally not renew the contract of an employee who has been here 20 years? After all, employment is year to year, isn't it? A principal may ask, "Can I legally dismiss this student? We don't really have much in the way of discipline records, but I remember several incidents." A teacher, being pressured by a student or parents to let the student do extra work to change a grade so the student is eligible for athletics or extra-curricular activities, may legitimately ask, "If I let one student do this, shouldn't every other student in the class have the same opportunity to submit extra work? Is it legal, let alone fair, to let one student and not the rest do something?" In this scenario, "Can I do this legally?" is not the only appropriate question; decision-making based solely on whether the proposed action is legal is incomplete and flawed. Instead, one should ask, "Given what the law permits and the Gospel demands, what should I do?"—a very different question.

There are often no easy answers for complex situations. Civil law may permit persons be treated in one way but conscience may demand another. It is true that Catholic parishes, schools and programs are businesses, but they are more than that—they are ministries undertaken for the sake of the Gospel.

Why not simply get rid of a problem employee? It will certainly be easier than having the annoyance of him or her on the staff another year. Terminating an employee or declining to renew a contract, in the absence of discriminatory intent or some violation of existing law, is perfectly legal, and if the analysis or reflection ends there, some would argue that what is legal is the right thing to do.

Contracts, if they exist at all, are year to year in Catholic parishes and schools. Unless there is a union contract (which few dioceses have and generally applies only to teachers), teachers have no legal expectation of continuing employment. Once the contract expires, it is entirely up to the individuals as to whether another agreement will be executed for the next year. Many employees do not have contracts; most states have "at will" employment laws-- persons can be terminated and no reason given. Even if a person has a contract and is terminated during the contract term, the most that an employee can expect, except in very unusual circumstances, is payment for the remainder of the contract.

In the absence of contracts, employees have no legal right to their jobs. A principal can walk into her secretary's office and say, "I'm sorry, but you are terminated as of today. Please vacate this office and remove your belongings by noon." Attorneys often advise this type of notification because anything you say can be used against you. So, if a principal were to say to a secretary, "I know it's hard for you to deliver messages upstairs so many times a day since you had a heart attack. I need somebody who can take the stairs without problems," the terminated secretary probably has an excellent case for discrimination on the basis of disability.

Approach is often everything. The principal could say, "I have some very difficult news. We are no longer able to employ you. We will give you two months' severance and will continue your benefits for those two months. I will do what I can to assist you in finding a new job." The employee at least should feel that the principal has some compassion and sense of fairness. Do you have to give someone two months' severance? Of course not. How would the principal want to be treated if the situation were reversed? Is there a good way to fire an employee or dismiss a student? Probably not. However, some approaches are far more compassionate than others.

Dismissing employees or not renewing their contracts generally becomes common knowledge fairly quickly. The details of the dismissal or non renewal may not be accurately reported, but the fact of the dismissal or non-renewal will be. It is easy for other employees to judge the administrator as heartless and unfeeling; the administrator can say little, if anything in his or her defense due to personnel policies, right to privacy laws and fear of litigation. So, teachers and other employees may believe that ethical and legal conflicts are the domain of administrators, not the ones in the trenches with the students.

Teacher and Staff Dilemmas

Let's return to the scenario involving the student who wants the grade in a class changed so that he or she will not be suspended from a team or activity. It is certainly possible for two reasonable teachers, each sincerely trying to do the right thing, to make different decisions—one may accept the extra work, while the other will not. Is one right and the other wrong? While the law may be black and white, ethical codes do not seem to be so.

Or consider the secretary who also serves as the attendance officer. A good student who is very conscientious returns after an absence and forgets her parental note. School rules allow one-day grace period. The next day the horrified student comes in and says, "I can't believe I did this. I forgot to ask my mother to write a note again. Please let me stay in school. The baby is sick and my mom won't be able to bring a note. Plus, she will be very angry."

If the rule states that a student who does not produce a note on the second day cannot go to classes, the specified action is clear. The secretary feels compassion for the student and whispers, "I'll let it go this time. Just be sure you have it tomorrow." Is that fair or just or ethical? The secretary could have sought out an administrator and asked for an exception for the student, but she didn't. What happens if tomorrow another student, not so conscientious, makes the same request? Has the secretary set a precedent?

These scenarios illustrate ethical and legal dilemmas. What can a person do when caught in the throes of such a dilemma? The first action would be to defer a decision pending time for thought and prayer. Many a person has hastily agreed to a course of action that soon proves to be unwise. One should always ask one's self, "What do I really believe about situations like this? Why would I agree to the request? Is it because I identify with the student? Why would I not agree? Is it because I don't like this student? Such dilemmas call for fearless self-examination and honesty. If a person is having trouble making or implementing a decision, a trusted person can be consulted.

The author remembers once having a graduate student plagiarize two major papers; she discovered the plagiarism by entering a few sentences into an Internet search engine. The student, a single mother, had risen from abject poverty to a very responsible position in her profession. She was viewed as a real success story and the author personally liked and admired her. The stated and published penalty for plagiarism of a major paper in graduate school was dismissal from the program for academic dishonesty, and the student had plagiarized two papers. After a few hours of prayer and argument with herself, she called one of her best friends, also a professor at the university, although in another academic department. The author explained the situation and the dire consequences that would accrue to the student if she "turned her in." Her friend listened, asked a few clarifying questions, but made no comments. The author said, "I know what the policy is. I know what she did. But she has had a very hard life and still has great responsibilities. The stress must have gotten to her. I need to find a way that I cannot turn her in and still do the right thing. I can't do this to her." To which her friend responded, "Are you responsible for her plagiarism? If she had asked for a time extension or an incomplete, would you have given it to her? Why will you be responsible if she has to take the consequences of her actions? And if you do not "turn her in," are you not setting a precedent that while plagiarism is wrong at the university, if you have a good enough excuse, you can avoid the consequences?" In the face of the questions, the author quickly saw that she was trying to find another honorable way out of a situation to which there was only one honorable course of action. She knew her friend would tell her the truth rather than tell her what he thought she wanted to hear. Would the author have found an excuse to not report the student? Probably not, but temptation can be very strong to bend the rules for someone with a sad story or someone that the teacher personally likes.

In the non-public sector, the law is generally on the side of the institution, unless it is clear that a law or legal responsibility has been breached since contract law governs agreements between parties in the private sector. Catholic school educators do not have to be concerned with the Constitutional rights of parents, students and teachers because such rights do not exist in a Catholic institution. Educators may believe that they are a law unto themselves and can take actions that might appear arbitrary to others. Private sector litigants often learn to their dismay that they will not get their positions back or their children returned to the school.   It can be truthfully said that one leaves one's Constitutional rights at the door when entering a Catholic school or program. Reinstatement of a dismissed teacher or student is usually not an option. The remedy for breach of contract is damages, not reinstatement. But does being able to do something without having to worry that a court might require the school to reinstate the individual, make the action right? Does the action hold people to standards they did not know existed? Would Jesus change the rules mid-stream or add new ones without notification?

Some years ago, the author was conducting a "beginning of the year" workshop for high school faculty. Arriving early, she heard the principal explain to the faculty that he was "taking back" a student who had been dismissed the previous year. He stated that the student appeared to have changed, to have accepted responsibility for his actions, and to deserve a second chance. Could the principal have legally kept the student out of school and terminated the relationship? Of course. Should the principal have kept him out? The principal struggled to make the right decision. No doubt, he prayed. He knew he was risking faculty displeasure and the possibility that the student might fail. But he chose to do what he thought was right, even though an easier, perfectly legal alternative existed. Similarly, a teacher can "throw" a disorderly student out of class or make the harder decision to work with that child to achieve a more harmonious relationship.

A Model for Legal/Ethical Decision Making

It's fairly easy to identify legal principles and decide what one can and cannot do. It is not so easy to decide what one should do in a relationship. The question should not be, "Is this what we *can* do?" but rather, "Is this what we *should* do? Is this what Jesus would do?" One way to reflect on issues and decisions is to use a legal/ethical decision-making model. Five steps are offered:

- Gather all relevant information
- Identify legal issues
- Identify moral/ethical/Gospel issues
- List and consider possible courses of action
- Choose one based on what is legal and right

In today's busy world, it is very easy to jump right into the "action" part, and neglect the two bookends of the model—prayer. Once prayer is forgotten or deferred, it becomes easier to neglect prayer the next time. Yet, in a Catholic school with a mission of teaching as Jesus did, how can we neglect to talk things over with the One in whose ministry we are engaged?

It is tempting to identify the legal issues and forget the rest. All involved with Catholic education in any form must remember that they are dealing with relationships—with God and with one another. Those with responsibility for the lives of others should always ask, "Is this the right thing to do? Do I have any other less painful alternatives? How will I feel about this decision in a year? Ten years? Is this what I would want done to me, if I were in this situation? Is this what Jesus would do?"

The remaining chapters of the book each present a short discussion of a legal issue followed by Reflection and Discussion questions. Readers are asked to consider both legal and ethical aspects of the issue before responding to the questions.

Chapter Two

WHAT DOES CIVIL LAW REQUIRE?

CONSTITUTIONAL LAW IS ONE OF THE MAJOR components of civil law in the United States today and is the main source of the law for the public school. In the majority of public school student and teacher dismissal cases, plaintiffs allege deprivation of constitutional rights. Catholic educators are probably familiar with certain constitutional rights. The First Amendment guarantees freedom of speech, press, assembly, and religion; the Fourth Amendment protects against unlawful searches and seizures; the Fifth and Fourteenth Amendments guarantee due process.

Public school teachers and students can claim constitutional rights because the public school is a government agency, and those who administer public schools are government agents. The Constitution protects persons from arbitrary governmental deprivation of their constitutional freedoms. Persons in Catholic schools, however, cannot claim such protections because Catholic schools are private institutions administered by private persons. These restrictions may seem unfair, yet a similar price is paid by anyone who works in a private institution. If a person goes to work in a supermarket, the person will probably be required to wear a uniform. The employee will not be permitted to wear a button advertising a different supermarket chain. First Amendment protections do not exist for supermarket employees.

The bottom line is that when one enters a private institution such as a Catholic school, one voluntarily surrenders the protections of the Constitution. A Catholic schoolteacher or student can always leave the Catholic school, but so long as the person remains in the institution, constitutional protections are not available. Thus, the Catholic school does not have to accept behaviors about which the public school has no choice, and even is required to protect.

What cannot lawfully be done in a public school may be done in a Catholic school. As stated earlier, the First Amendment to the Constitution protects persons' rights to free speech; therefore, administrators in public schools may not make rules prohibiting the expression of an unpopular viewpoint. Unless there is clear evidence of possible disruption or harm resulting from the expression of an unpopular viewpoint.

Most educators have heard of the 1969 landmark United States Supreme Court decision *Tinker v. DesMoines Independent School District* that produced the now famous line, "Neither students or teachers shed their constitutional rights at the [public] schoolhouse gate." Since no such constitutional protection exists in the Catholic School, administrators may restrict the speech of both students and teachers.

Fairness and Due Process

Public schools must be concerned with constitutional issues. Catholic schools, while not bound to grant constitutional freedoms per se, are bound to act in a manner characterized by fairness. Some legal experts talk about a "smell" test. If an action "smells" wrong when a person examines it, it may be suspect. In the end, the actions expected of Catholic schools may appear much like constitutional protections. In no area is this more evident than in due process considerations.

The Fifth Amendment to the Constitution guarantees the federal government will not deprive someone of "life, liberty, or property without due process of law." The Fourteenth Amendment made the Fifth Amendment and all other amendments in the Bill of Rights applicable to all states. Persons entitled to constitutional due process have substantive due process rights, property interests (that can be the subject of ownership, including jobs and education) and liberty interests (freedom, reputation). Substantive due process involves moral as well as legal ramifications: Is this action fair and reasonable? Substantive due process applies whenever property or liberty interests can be shown.

The Constitution also guarantees procedural due process; in other words, how a deprivation occurs. In the public school, procedural due process includes *notice* (a presentation of the allegations against the accused); *hearing* (an opportunity to respond); *before an impartial tribunal* (an opportunity to *confront* and *cross-examine* accusers); and an opportunity to call *witnesses in one's own behalf.* In serious disciplinary cases, a person in the public school has the right to have an attorney present.

Procedural due process has been defined as a question: What process is due? In the public sector, several elements are present. In meeting the requirements of fairness, Catholic school educators should ask themselves these questions:

- What are our disciplinary procedures?
- Are they reasonable?
- Are all the students treated fairly and, as far as reasonably possible, in the same way?
- Are there clear procedures that students and parents can expect will be followed?

Catholic schools, while not bound to provide the whole panoply of procedural due process protections that public schools must provide, are nonetheless expected to be fair. Ohio Court of Appeals in 1979 ruled in a Catholic school discipline case held that courts could intervene in private school disciplinary cases if "the proceedings do not comport with fundamental fairness" (*Geraci v. St. Xavier High School*). Fundamental fairness in a Catholic school is akin to, but not synonymous with, constitutional due process in the public school.

Federal and State Statutes

Federal and state statutes and regulations, many of which reflect theories of constitutional law, comprise a second source of the law affecting Catholic schools and their personnel. If a statute requires that all who operate an educational institution within a given state follow a certain directive, both Catholic and public schools are bound. So long as what is required does not unfairly impinge upon the rights of Catholic schools and can be shown to have some legitimate educational purpose, Catholic schools can be compelled to comply with state legislative requirements. The only situation in which a Catholic school can be required to grant federal constitutional protections occurs when state action can be found to be so pervasive within the school that the school can be fairly said to be acting as an agent of an individual state. The key factor in state action is the nexus or relationship between the state and the challenged activity. Although litigants have alleged state action in Catholic schools, no court of record to date has found state action present in private school teacher or student dismissal cases.

In a 1982 teacher dismissal case, *Rendell-Baker v. Kohn*, the United States Supreme Court ruled that a dismissal from a private school reception of 90-99% of its funding from the state did not constitute state action. *Rendell-Baker* seems to render the state action issue moot in cases alleging violation of constitutional due process protections. A different situation can exist in cases alleging violations of federal anti-discrimination and civil rights legislation. In those cases, the presence of federal funding can result in an institution's being required to abide by the legislation.

Since Catholic schools are not bound to grant constitutional protections unless significant state action is found, litigants alleging a denial of constitutional due process will have to prove the existence of significant state action within the institution before the court will grant relief. It is very important for Catholic school educators to keep these facts in mind.

It is not uncommon for parents, students or teachers to claim that their constitutional rights have been violated in the Catholic school when, in fact, no constitutional rights ever existed in the first place. These realities need to be clarified very early in a relationship between a Catholic school and its staff, students and parents. One way to prevent possible misunderstandings is to develop and disseminate comprehensive handbooks that outline the rights and responsibilities of all persons in the Catholic school.

Guidelines

The beginning point for rules development should be the school's philosophy and mission. All students can be brought to some understanding of institutional philosophy: "At our school we try to treat each other the way Jesus would." The life of the school should be seen as flowing from its philosophy.

Rules should be clear and understandable. The test that might be applied by the court is: Would two persons of average intelligence reading this rule have the same understanding of it? A rule stating, "Students arriving at class after the bell will be marked tardy" is clear, while a rule such as "Late students will be marked tardy" is open to such questions as: How late is late? After the bell? After the teacher begins class? Whenever possible, rules should be written. It is easier to refer to the written rule when emotions run high than to insist, "at the beginning of the school year this rule was announced." Courts look for evidence of good faith: Did the institution have a rule promulgated? Did the student know of the rule? The court does not concern itself with the wisdom of the rule or even with the rightness or wrongness of the professional opinion of educators; the court is only concerned with the existence of a properly promulgated rule and with the institution's acting in good faith according to state procedures. Courts look for basic fairness in the execution of the contract existing between the student/parent and the school, when the student/parent alleges that a school acted improperly.

Educators must understand that it is impossible to identify everything a student might do that could result in discipline, including suspension or expulsion. Therefore, it is advisable to have some kind of "catch-all" clause such as "other inappropriate conduct" or "conduct, whether inside or outside the school, that is detrimental to the reputation of the school." No court will expect a school to have listed all possible offenses, but courts will expect that there are written rules and that students and parents have a reasonable idea of the expectations of the school.

Every school should have some written handbook. Parents should be required to sign a form stating that they have read the rules and agree to be governed by them. Handbooks are discussed in greater detail in Chapter Fourteen. When considering the development of student guidelines, educators should be aware that there is a time investment involved. If a teacher allows a student to tell his or her story instead of summarily imposing punishment—for example, making all students whose names are on the board remain after school—the teacher makes a commitment to spending time with a student who faces discipline. The principal or disciplinarian makes a commitment to listening to the student's side of the story as well as to the teacher's, but the benefit should be obvious: students perceive teachers and administrators as trying to be fair and, hopefully, will internalize the values modeled.

Somewhat more extensive procedures should be developed if the penalty is suspension. One-day suspensions, at minimum, require the involvement of the principal, assistant principal or dean of students. Students should never be suspended until parents are notified. Under no circumstances should students be sent home during the school day to begin a suspension. Longer suspensions should involve a written notice of the charges and a hearing. From an ethical if not a legal standpoint, cases in which the possibility of expulsion exist should require both formal notification and a hearing at which the student normally should be able to confront accusers. Careful documentation must be kept in all major disciplinary proceedings. There is no requirement, however, that a student be allowed to have legal counsel present at any stage of the Catholic school's disciplinary proceedings. The guiding principle in any consideration of student rights and discipline should be the desire to act in a Christian manner characterized by fairness and compassion.

FOR REFLECTION AND DISCUSSION

- Student C is angry with you for giving her a detention because she was wearing an article of clothing in violation of the dress code and/or uniform rules. She tells you that she has a First Amendment right to freedom of expression. How will you respond?
- Student Y questions you in class: "Don't you think the administration is wrong in searching lockers? Lockers should be private. A few of us are thinking about having a protest the next time the vice-principal tries to search our lockers? After all the stuff in there is ours. So, what can they do to us if we don't let them search? They can't throw us out for that, can they?" How will you answer?
- Student K has asked you at the beginning of class, "So, do we have any rights in a Catholic school?" What will you say?

Chapter Three

HOW CATHOLIC DO WE
HAVE TO BE?

Note: This chapter first appeared in the March 2004 edition of NCEA Notes and reprinted in the book Compendium of NCEA NOTES "LEGAL ISSUES" Articles: 1990-2007. Reflection and discussion questions have since been added.

TODAY'S CATHOLIC EDUCATORS TALK a great deal about Catholic identity. What makes a school Catholic? How does a school claim its Catholic heritage? What do we have to do to be Catholic? Do we have to agree with everything the Church says? What should I say if a student asks me what I think and I don't agree with the Church's position? Isn't it dishonest to support a position you think is wrong? These are all questions that most readers will have heard. The writer hears them on a weekly, sometimes daily, basis. This chapter will attempt to offer some answers from a legal perspective.

What Makes a School Catholic?

Simply calling an institution Catholic does not make it so. Being Catholic requires a commitment to the Gospel, the teachings of Jesus Christ and the teachings of the Roman Catholic Church, both when it is convenient to be committed and when it is not so convenient. If any of the above is compromised, the school is eroding its Catholicity, but one can legitimately argue that being Catholic is an either/or proposition: either the school is Catholic or it isn't.

"Cafeteria" Approaches to Catholicism Not Permitted

In the 1970s, many in the Church talked about a cafeteria approach to Catholicism: "I like the church's teachings on social justice, so I'll support them. I think the Church is wrong about birth control, so I'll follow my conscience—after all, doesn't the Church teach that conscience is primary?" These statements are probably familiar to many readers.

However, there is one basic bottom line. A Catholic educator's first legal duty is to be true to the teachings of the Catholic Church. A Catholic educator is an agent of the Catholic Church and has to hold the "company line," as this author often states. The situation is similar to that of any person who works for any organization. If I work for a company that makes umbrellas, I have to uphold the company's products. I probably won't be employed very long if I encourage people to buy plastic rain hoods as an alternative to umbrellas. Perhaps the analogy seems a bit simplistic, but the underlying premise is not: if one cannot support the company that one works for and the products the company produces, the honest course of action is to find another job.

The product we are selling is Catholic education. Parents send their children to Catholic schools and religious education programs for Catholic education, not for the private opinions of teachers and catechists, and they have a legal right to expect fidelity to Church teaching.

Isn't Conscience Primary?

The Catholic Church does teach that one's conscience, properly formed, is primary. Nevertheless, the question of agency is still the "sticking point." If you teach in a Catholic school and your students ask your opinion about the Church's position on an issue, you are not at liberty to share your personal opinion with the students if that opinion is at odds with the Church's position. The teacher is an agent of the Church, the same way a bishop or the pope is an agent.

Sometimes, this reality is painful. The Church does not claim to be perfect, but persons who are responsible for the Catholic education of young persons must teach them the precepts of the Church as the Church has taught them, not as individual teachers might like them to be. To do less is to fail in one's primary legal obligation.

So What's an Educator to Do?

The Catholic educator must present the teachings of the Catholic Church. It is certainly permissible to say that some persons do not agree with whatever the teaching is, but one must be clear about what the church's position is. The educator is not free to say, for example, "I think the Church is wrong about birth control. Responsible persons use artificial contraception" or "Women should be ordained. The Pope is wrong." If pressed for one's personal opinion, one can say, "My personal opinion is not what we are discussing. The Church teaches. . ."

Issues of Lifestyle

There are certainly Catholic educators who are living in sexual relationships with others to whom they are not married. At the very least, if an individual's lifestyle becomes a matter of scandal, the administrator must address it. Teaching in a Catholic institution is not the same as having a job in industry. What the Catholic educator does both inside and outside the institution matters because he or she has chosen to be a role model for young people. The Catholic Church, its parishes and programs have the legal right to demand that its educators live lives and speak words consistent with the Church's teachings.

FOR REFLECTION AND DISCUSSION

• You are the moderator/advisor for the debate club. In a meeting with the club officers, the president informs you that the topic they wish to debate in the mock debates presented in the school before the team debates teams from other schools, is: "Should women have the right to have abortions?" The president says two students, star senior debaters, who strongly believe in a woman's right to choose have already volunteered to argue that position. The president also reports that, as it has been difficult to find persons to argue that women should not have a right to choose to have an abortion, he has assigned two freshmen to argue that position. What will you say? Will you agree to the school debate having that topic?

• A girl and her boyfriend stop by your classroom and ask if they can talk with you. They tell you that they have a problem and they cannot talk to their parents, the counselors, or the campus ministers, but that they have always considered you to be fair and a good thinker. They tell you that they began having sexual relations a few months ago; the girl was able to procure birth control pills without her parents' knowledge. She had a very bad reaction to the pills and she does not plan to take them again. So, they ask you, "How bad is it to use a condom— really? Isn't it better to prevent a birth than to have an abortion? We are not ready to be parents. Now, we know teachers preach abstinence, but how realistic is that? Please tell us that it is OK to use condoms." How will your respond?

Chapter Four

Personal Conduct of Staff Members

Personal Conduct

Educators, particularly administrators, often face issues of actual or perceived inappropriate staff conduct, and may wonder what legal rights they have to demand certain standards of behavior from staff, particularly during off-campus times. What a staff member does, both in and outside the educational setting, impacts the quality and integrity of ministry within the setting. The doctrine of separation of church and state protects administrators and allows them to set standards of personal behavior that would not be permitted in the public sector.

Behavioral Expectations for Catholic Educators and Ministers

Contracts and other documents governing employment and volunteer status should state that staff members are expected to support the teachings of the Catholic Church through their behavior. For example, if the fact that an individual had an abortion becomes known and is a source of scandal, the school and/or parish has every right to terminate that individual's employment or volunteer status. To do otherwise might send a confusing message to parents, students, and the larger community.

Issues of Sexual Preference and/or Lifestyle

Issues of sexual preference and lifestyle pose special problems. While no one should condemn a homosexual orientation, a Catholic administrator as an agent of the Church, cannot ignore manifestations of an openly gay lifestyle that pose scandal. Persons of the opposite sex who are romantically involved and are living together, but not married, pose difficulties as well. This author believes that the best approach may be to simply reiterate the church's teaching that all sex outside marriage is wrong.

Equally difficult decisions must be made in situations involving divorced staff members who remarry without an annulment if that fact becomes known. Even if the individual in question is convinced that he or she is acting in good conscience in contracting a second marriage, there is little doubt that the person is, objectively speaking, in violation of church law and hence, a possible source of scandal. The situation is not a problem from the standpoint of terminating the employment of a person who violates church law. Religious entities clearly can terminate the employment of one who violates religious norms. The problem is the lack of consistency from diocese to diocese, from parish to parish, and sometimes even within the same parish. All persons and institutions are expected to be fair. How can an employer claim to be fair in dealings with employees and volunteers if one is treated one way and a second another way for the same behavior, depending on whom is involved? It is difficult to defend dismissal decisions on religious grounds if one person is dismissed for an action and another, having acted in the same manner, is retained. These principles hold in any case involving religious issues. There is no easy solution but governing boards and administrators have an obligation to see that the teachings of the Catholic Church are respected and not compromised in the witness given by staff members. Many dioceses have policies concerning scandalous public behavior.

In summary, once an individual performs an act that is inconsistent with Church teaching and that act becomes publicly known, the person may no longer be qualified to teach or minister at that time. While such a reality may seem obvious, it is recommended that documents state the requirement of supporting the teachings of the Church.

Illegal Activity

A person who has committed an illegal act may certainly have employment or volunteer status terminated. One who is convicted of, or who admits commission of, a crime should be removed from professional and/or volunteer status. The harder question arises when a person is simply accused of, or arrested on suspicion of, a crime. Administrators may be sharply divided as to the proper response to make in such a situation.

The United States has long operated under the principle of "innocent until proven guilty." It may appear that, until guilt is established, the fair approach would be to let the person continue in his or her position. Yet, the reality often is that effectiveness in such situations is severely compromised.

How, then, should the administrator deal with an arrest of, or serious accusation concerning, a paid or volunteer staff member? Every parish and school should have a policy in place that allows the administrator to place the accused individual on a leave of absence pending the outcome of an investigation or an adjudication of guilt. How will the other employees respond to another staff member's being accused of a crime? How will they deal with the inevitable student questions, once the story appears in the newspaper and/or on the nightly news?

While no one likes to think about a colleague being arrested and/or accused of a crime or serious misconduct, it might be advisable to consider how one might respond in such a situation even if the situation never arises? Once a person makes a statement, it is difficult to "take it back" even if one has reconsidered and/or realized that the words said were spoken in haste. Even if the accused is guilty, he or she is a person with dignity.

FOR REFLECTION AND DISCUSSION

- You have just learned that one of your female colleagues has acknowledged that the woman with whom she lives is her lover and that they were married in Vermont, a state that permits and recognizes same sex marriages. When asked a direct question by the principal, she answered truthfully. The principal told her that she would have to resign by the end of the week or be terminated. You know that one of your male colleagues is in a similar relationship with his roommate. Will you tell the principal about the male colleague's situation? What will you say if the principal should ask you?

- Assume that the bishop of your diocese has recently mandated that females may no longer function as altar servers. You are in charge of the next school Mass at which a priest from a neighboring parish has agreed to preside. You know that there is little chance that the priest would report female servers to the bishop, unless asked directly by him. In fact, you think there is little likelihood that anyone would say anything. Girls have always served at school Masses and they want to serve now. What will you do? How will you explain your decision to them?

Chapter Five

Negligence: What Is it and How Can We Avoid It?

THE SEXUAL ABUSE CRISIS in the Catholic Church has raised the anxiety level of most persons who work in Catholic schools and other ministries. Administrators, teachers and others rightfully fear both the inconvenience and the expense of litigation. Educators should understand that if a school administrator or teacher is sued, there is a high degree of probability that the suit will allege negligence. Even though negligence is an issue, the avoidance of which necessitates high educator vigilance, it is often the most difficult type of case about which to predict an accurate judicial outcome. What may be considered negligence in one court may not be so considered in another. It is much better, obviously, to avoid being accused of negligence in the first place than to take one's chances on the outcome of a lawsuit.

Often, though, educators are misinformed about some of the greatest problem areas. While sexual abuse cases claim the headlines, the vast majority of cases involving teachers are not ones alleging sexual abuse; rather, the most often-litigated cases are ones alleging negligence. Black's Law Dictionary (1999) defines negligence as, "failure to exercise the standard of care that a reasonably prudent person would have exercised in a similar situation" (p. 1056). There are two types of negligence: one type is omission, the failure to do what should have been done and the second type is commission, the doing of something that led to an injury. Everyone who works with young persons needs to learn the lessons of negligence law.

Teachers, rather than principals, are most often present when something goes wrong, someone is injured, and a lawsuit is filed. Pastors and administrators can find themselves named in lawsuits as well, under the doctrine of *respondeat superior*, let the superior answer. This doctrine allows courts to hold the superiors of negligent persons liable for the employee's negligence. Teachers have a right to expect that principals will give them the information they need to avoid negligence. Teachers have a responsibility as well: to use common sense and to act the way one would expect a reasonable, mature teacher to act. Courts also expect that policies and procedures will be in place, and that teachers will be familiar with those policies and procedures and will follow them. Administrators are expected to supervise teachers. Sometimes, teachers may chafe under supervision and feel that the administrator doesn't trust them when in fact, supervision is a teacher's best defense against a charge of malpractice. If an administrator can say that the teacher acted appropriately when observed, a powerful piece of evidence is added in the teacher's favor.

All educators should be familiar with the elements of negligence. Four elements must be present before a finding of legal negligence can be made and those elements are: duty, violation of duty, proximate cause and injury. If one of these elements is missing, legal negligence cannot be found. Since negligence is an unintentional act, which results in an injury, a person charged with negligence is generally not going to face criminal charges or spend time in prison. An examination of each of the four elements necessary to constitute a finding of negligence should be helpful.

The first element is duty. Students have a right to safety, and teachers and principals have a responsibility to protect the safety of all entrusted to their care. Teachers are expected to provide reasonable supervision of students. Administrators should develop rules and regulations, which guide teachers in providing for student safety, and teachers should develop classroom procedures, which protect student safety. Teachers will generally not be held responsible for injuries occurring at a place where, or at a time when, they had no responsibility. A student injured on the way to school, for example, normally will not be able to demonstrate that a teacher or administrator had a duty to protect the student. If a teacher is walking through a mall on Sunday afternoon and sees two students fighting, he has no duty to intervene since he is not part of the mall security force. However, concern for his students or for the reputation of the school may prompt him to intervene in an attempt to stop the fight. He may feel he has a moral or legal obligation to intervene. Once, he takes action, he has assumed a duty he was not leally required to assume. His becoming involved results in his assuming a legal duty.

When considering the concept of duty, it is important to keep in mind that the court will look at the reasonableness of the educator's behavior. A commonly asked question is, "Did the teacher do what a reasonable teacher would be expected to do?"

The second element is violation of duty. Negligence cannot exist if the supervising educator has not violated a duty. Courts expect that accidents and spontaneous actions can occur. If a teacher is properly supervising a playground at recess, and one child throws a rock at another child and causes an injury, the teacher cannot be held liable if she had no reason to know or suspect that the child was likely to throw a rock. However, if a teacher who is responsible for the supervision of the playground were to allow rock throwing to continue without attempting to stop it and a student were injured, the teacher would probably be held liable. Similarly, a teacher who leaves a classroom unattended in order to take a coffee break will generally be held to have violated a duty. But if it can be demonstrated that teachers have, as a general practice, taken coffee breaks and left classes unattended, and, because of the inattention or inaction of the principal, nothing was done about the situation, the principal may be held equally, if not more, liable than the teacher.

If a teacher takes a group of six-year-olds to a lake and leaves them unsupervised for an hour, her action would be viewed as professional negligence. Nonetheless, if no injury results from the person's action, as will be discussed later, there can be no finding of legal negligence. Thus, legal negligence must be distinguished from professional negligence, which is definitely demonstrated by leaving children unattended. Courts expect that persons will take reasonable precautions to ensure that accidents will not happen. Courts have consistently said that there is no requirement that the teacher foresee the specific type of accident, but merely the possibility of some danger. However, violation of duty in one instance may not result in a finding of legal negligence if a causal connection, proximate cause, between the violation and the injury cannot be shown or if no injury was incurred.

The third element of negligence is proximate cause. Proximate cause is a contributing factor that "makes or breaks" negligence claim. If the supervisor had done what should have been done, there would have been no injury, or if the supervisor had not done the thing that was done, there would have been no injury. The arguably old but still very relevant Minnesota case of *Levandoski v. Jackson City School District*, decided in 1976, illustrates. A teacher failed to report a student as missing from her class. The student was later found murdered some distance from the school. She had also been sexually assaulted. The child's parents alleged that, if the absence had been properly and promptly reported, the murder could have been prevented. Clearly, the teacher had a duty to know who was present and to report those who should have been present and were not. She violated that duty. The court ruled, nonetheless, that the parents had failed to prove that had the absence been reported, the assault and murder could have been prevented. Thus, the claim failed for a lack of proximate cause. One should not conclude that carelessness of reporting an absence is not a serious matter. If the facts were changed to a situation in which the student was found murdered on the school grounds or in the school building, a different judgment might have been given since it would be much more likely that the report might have prevented the injuries.

One of the most well known Catholic school negligence cases is *Smith v. the Archbishop of St. Louis* decided in 1982. A second grade teacher kept a lighted candle to honor the Blessed Mother on her desk during the month of May. She admitted under oath that she gave the children no special instructions regarding candles and/or fires. On a day during which a play was to be presented, the Smith child, wearing a crepe paper costume, walked too close to the fire. Her costume caught on fire, and she was severely injured, particularly in the facial area. Her scars and disfigurement are permanent. The child sustained psychological damage and experts testified that she would likely experience a lifetime of psychological problems. Clearly, the teacher's violation of duty in placing a lighted candle within reach of seven year olds was a contributing factor and constituted proximate cause.

In this case, the Missouri Appellate Court discussed the concept of *foreseeability*. The plaintiff did not have to prove that the defendant could foresee a particular injury—the plaintiff's costume catching fire—had to occur. The plaintiff had to establish that a reasonable person would have foreseen that injuries could result from having an unattended lighted candle in a second grade classroom, particularly when no safety instructions had been given to the students. It is often difficult to predict what a court will consider proximate cause in any particular allegation of negligence. Although Smith bound only Missouri and the other states reporting in the southwest report, the principles of negligence are the same across the United States.

The fourth element of negligence is injury. No matter how irresponsible the behavior of a teacher or administrator, if there is no injury, there can be no legal negligence. This reality is surprising to some people. The purpose of litigation is to be made whole, restored to as similar a condition existing prior to the injury as possible. Injuries do not have to be physical; they can be psychological, mental, and academic as well. Many cases do not allege physical injury, but seek damages for emotional distress, particularly when that distress can be demonstrated. There are two causes of action alleging emotional distress. One is negligent infliction of emotional distress which generally requires that there be physical symptoms of emotional distress. Intentional infliction of emotional distress, while harder to prove, of course, does not require physical manifestations of the distress.

Most negligence cases occur in the classroom because that is where students and teachers spend most of their time. However, there are other areas that are potentially more dangerous than the classroom and, hence, a greater standard of care will be expected. Lab and physical education classes, for example, carry greater potential for injury, and case law indicates that courts expect teachers to exercise greater caution than they would in ordinary classrooms. Teachers and administrators are expected to maintain equipment in working order and to keep areas free of unnecessary hazards. Teachers should also give students safety instructions regarding the use of potentially dangerous equipment.

The younger the child, the greater the teacher's responsibility. It might be acceptable to leave a group of high school seniors alone in a math classroom for a good reason when it would not be acceptable to leave a group of first graders alone. It is reasonable to expect that fifteen-year-olds of average intelligence could observe traffic signals when crossing a street. It would not be reasonable to expect kindergarten children to do so.

FOR REFLECTION AND DISCUSSION

- Do I have rules for classroom behavior? Are they posted? Have I discussed them with students? Are my rules clear and consistently enforced? Do I understand that children's safety is more important than how the students feel about me on any given day?
- While you are teaching a class, two students appear and tell you that Student B has somehow gotten his hand stuck in the ice cream machine in the student lounge. No other teachers or staff members are nearby. You have twenty-five students in your class, and no way to contact the office. What will you do?
- You supervised a student trip to a nursing home. One student was visiting an elderly couple who had a large window; the student opened the window and attempted to jump to his death. He landed in a gutter where he was eventually rescued by firefighters, but he sustained a broken ankle from the attempt. His parents are talking about suing you on the grounds that you should have foreseen this type of injury and taken plans to avoid it. What do you think? Are you negligent or not?

Chapter Six

STUDENT PRIVACY AND REPUTATION: BALANCING RIGHTS WHILE AVOIDING HARM

PRIVACY AND REPUTATION are two serious legal issues facing Catholic educators today. Both students and teachers expect that information concerning them will be revealed only to those with a right to know. School officials who fail to take reasonable measures to safeguard such information could face civil lawsuits for defamation of character.

Defamation of Character

Defamation is an unprivileged communication that harms the reputation of another. Defamation, which may involve invasion of privacy, can be either spoken, slander, or written, libel.

Educators should be concerned with protecting the reputations of all in their schools. Educators should exercise great care in keeping student and teacher records, as well as in speaking about student behavior. It is only just that an educator refrains from gossip or unnecessary derogatory remarks about other teachers and/or students. The best advice for Catholic educators is to be as factual as possible in official documents and to refrain from "editorial" comments. Whatever is written should meet the following three criteria. Comments should be:

- Specific
- Behaviorally-oriented
- Verifiable (for example, someone else could have observed the behavior)

It is more professional, and legally more appropriate, to write, "Bobby has been absent four times this month, late for class eight times, and sent to the principal's office for fighting five times," than to write, "Bobby is absent too much, late most of the time, and always in trouble." It is better to write, "Susan is reading on a first-grade level" than to write, "Susan can't read."

If there is no reason to have an item in a student's file, it should be stored elsewhere. Disciplinary records, in particular, should not be stored in official files. Students are still in a formative stage, and school officials should exercise extreme caution in storing information that could be harmful to a student. Disciplinary records should not be a part of the information sent to another school when a student transfers or graduates. If the new school requires disciplinary information, the transferring school should consider preparing a document containing the information and having the parents sign a statement that they have seen the document and agree to its being sent.

Recommendations

In today's litigious society, most educators are familiar with the problems of writing legally non-controversial recommendations for students without sacrificing the truth. Further, most teachers have read recommendations that seem to say very little. All educators must understand that no one has an absolute, legal right to a recommendation; however, fairness would seem to indicate that only the most extreme situations should result in a student being denied a recommendation.

College recommendations pose particular problems. For example, a student or parent may demand a recommendation from a certain teacher if the recommendation must come from a teacher in a given discipline. If a teacher were to decline to write the recommendation, the parent would probably simply complain to the principal and/or guidance department head and the teacher may become involved in a battle. Therefore, the following approach is recommended when writing recommendations for students who cannot be recommended.

Students can be given letters verifying enrollment and factual statements can be made about education and participation in extra-curricular activities. The guideline is to be as fair as possible. School officials should strive to be fair and respectful of the dignity of others in all communications, whether official or not, and to say only what can be shown to have some valid relationship to the professional situation. In so doing, school officials protect themselves against possible lawsuits alleging defamation and/or invasion of privacy.

Secondary school teachers may presume that a waiver of the right to read a recommendation is absolute, but it is not. Such a waiver is only as good as the custodian of the records. It is not unheard of for a student or parent to contact a college office and ask why a student was not admitted, and be read the recommendation. A teacher can always argue that this is his or her honest opinion, as well it may be. The above-mentioned procedures should help, though, in fairly and compassionately attempting to meet students' needs without compromising fairness.

Confidentiality of Records

An issue related to invasion of privacy is confidentiality of records. If an educator follows the procedures outlined above, the risk of having problematic materials in student files is minimized. The contents of student files should be released only to authorized persons. Even faculty and staff should be given access to student files only for appropriate, school-related reasons. Parental signatures should be required before records are sent to anyone.

Older educators in Catholic schools can recall when neither they nor students' parents were permitted access to their student records. In 1975 the Buckley Amendment granted students and parents the right to inspect school records, was passed by Congress. Some legal experts believe that the Buckley Amendment does not apply to private schools. The amendment contains a clause that provides that the legislation does not apply to private schools solely because of the presence of government funds (for example, federal commodities in cafeterias, bloc grant money and so forth). However, this belief has never been tested in court.

There are cases in which private sector officials have been required to comply with federal legislation, such as anti-discrimination statutes. The requirement was based on public policy considerations, commonly accepted standards of behavior. It is better to comply *voluntarily* with legislation such as the Buckley Amendment than to risk becoming a test case for the courts. Legalities aside, it seems only right that persons affected by records have the right to see them.

FOR REFLECTION AND DISCUSSION

- Student Y, who has a D average in your class, asks you to write a recommendation for her to a highly competitive program in a top tier college. You believe she has virtually no chance of success. However, if you refuse to write the recommendation, you know there will be fallout. If you write truthfully, you believe there is a good chance that her mother, an alumna and local politician, will find out what you wrote. How will you respond? Will you write the recommendation?

- Tommy Smith is a student who works very hard to get barely passing grades. You have a great rapport with Tommy. He has applied to a small college that has just announced that due to a completely unexpected surge in applicants, the school will be unable to accept around 50% of those who apply. The college has a practice of admitting students with less than stellar high school records who have more ability than they use. You believe Tommy tries his hardest and uses his abilities and you are not convinced that he will succeed in his chosen college. Tommy gives you the recommendation form and asks you, please, to not say anything that would keep him out of the college. There are several questions dealing with working to potential and academic promise. The last question is, "Would you recommend that this applicant be accepted? Why or why not?" How will you respond?

Chapter Seven

STAFF AND STUDENT
RELATIONSHIPS

TEACHERS AND OTHER STAFF MEMBERS care about students. That care extends to all areas of student life. Educators often find themselves counseling students in personal matters; it is not unusual for a teacher to find him/herself in the position of "surrogate parent," once a fairly common experience, but now one that can be fraught with legal liability. Students often entrust teachers with confidential information. Teachers, many with little training in professional counseling, often question what is appropriate in interacting with students outside the classroom setting.

Few guidelines are available. Teachers and other personnel often deal with situations that pose personal and legal risks for the adults as well as for the students. This author is familiar with several situations in which parents threatened and/or pursued legal action against a teacher whose actions they viewed as unwise, inappropriate, sexually motivated or interfering with the parent/ child relationship. All adults working in the educational ministry of the church should be aware of the legal ramifications involved.

Allegations of Sexual Misconduct

One end of the student/staff relationship spectrum is represented by sexual misconduct. Sexual misconduct can be alleged in apparently innocent situations. Students can misinterpret touching, and a teacher could find him/herself facing child abuse charges. Extreme caution is in order whenever a teacher touches a student.

A student who believes that a teacher has not responded to efforts to achieve a closer relationship poses another kind of problem. Such a student may accuse a teacher of inappropriate conduct as a retaliatory measure. Educators must be aware that serious consequences can result from an allegation of child abuse, even if that allegation is eventually proven to be false. At the very least, such a false allegation can be extremely embarrassing for the teacher. If a child abuse report is made, authorities will question the teacher, keep a record of the investigation, and, in all likelihood, place the name of the accused on a list of alleged offenders.

Thus, it is imperative that educators protect themselves and the students they teach by practicing appropriate behavior with students. To avoid even the slightest hint of impropriety, a teacher should avoid being alone with a single student behind closed doors unless a window or other opening permits outsiders to see into the area. A good question to ask oneself might be: If this were my child, would I have any objection to a teacher relating with him or her in this manner?

Fear of teachers facing child abuse allegations has caused some public school districts in this country to adopt rules that prohibit any faculty touching of students. Such rules preclude putting one's arm around students, patting a student on the back, and giving a student a hug. No Catholic school educator would want to take such a position, but common sense precautions must be taken for the protection of all.

Other Physical Contact

Educators can also be charged with child abuse that is not sexual. Corporal punishment, prohibited by regulation in most Catholic schools, can set the stage for allegations of physical abuse. An example of punitive touching occurred when a teacher tapped a child on the shoulder with a folder while reprimanding the child for not having done his homework, The child's mother filed a child abuse report against the teacher and threatened to file charges of assault and battery. Although the case is outrageous, it does indicate the dangers that can exist. Thus, educators are well advised to adopt the operating rule: Never touch a child in a way that can be construed as punitive.

Other Behavior

Teachers and other staff members must bear in mind that they are professionals rendering a service. Just as a counselor or psychiatrist is professionally bound to avoid emotional involvement with a client, a teacher should strive to avoid becoming so emotionally involved with a student that objectivity and fairness are compromised. Teachers must remember that they have many students for whom they are responsible and who need and may desire the teacher's attention. If a relationship with a student keeps a teacher from responding to other student needs on a regular basis, the teacher should seriously examine the appropriateness of the relationship.

In seeking to assess the appropriateness of a teacher/student relationship, some mental health professionals recommend asking oneself questions such as these: Whose needs are being met? Is there a boundary? Where is it?

The following adult behaviors could be considered inappropriate, depending on the totality of the circumstances: dropping by a student's home, particularly if no parent is present; frequent telephoning of the student; social trips with a student; sharing of teacher's personal problems.

Serving as a Catholic educator in these times is a privilege and a gift. It is indeed sad when an educator is forced to relinquish that gift because of inappropriate choices. Reflection and prudent behavior will keep educators both legally protected and professionally fulfilled.

FOR REFLECTION AND DISCUSSION

- Student X, a member of the opposite sex, has been leaving little boyfriend/girlfriend cards on your desk and signing them "With all my heart and all my love." How will you respond?

- You are very worried about Jane, one of your students. She has told you that her parents are "never at home." They are quite wealthy and spend a great deal of time in Europe with a company they own there. There is a live-in maid but according to 14-year-old Jane, the maid speaks very little English, considers her responsibilities cleaning and cooking, and usually has her boyfriend spend the night with her when the parents aren't home. There are three younger children and Jane has become, at least according to her reports, the mother. She sees that they are up, dressed, fed (the maid is usually not up at breakfast time but leaves food on the counter and in the refrigerator) and on their way to school each morning. You have discussed your concerns with a few of your colleagues who have warned you against getting involved. In particular, they tell you that Child Protective Services will never intervene in a situation in which all the physical needs of the children are met. In October, you sent an e-mail to the parents asking for a conference. A secretary responded that the parents could meet you for thirty minutes on December 26 or December 31, but only if the matter was truly urgent and could not be handled by the maid. What will you do?

- You are particularly concerned with the well being of Student Z who appears to be ill clothed and under-nourished. He appears at the door of your home around 10 p.m. one evening. He wears only pajamas and says his father has thrown him out. He asks if he can stay with you. What would you answer?

Chapter Eight

AVOIDING THE APPEARANCE
OF IMPROPRIETY:
RECOMMENDATIONS FOR
KEEPING BOUNDARIES

TODAY EVERYONE SEEMS TO BE TALKING about boundaries and the avoidance of litigation prompted by the appearance of impropriety. Here is a truncated list of "do nots" for educators to follow:

1. **Do not stay alone in a room with a student unless there is a window permitting others to view the room or the door is open.**
    Think before you act. Ask yourself how someone else might perceive what you are doing. If a student were to leave your classroom or other area and claim abuse, a closed area with no visual access would leave little room for a defense.

2. **Do not allow students to become overly friendly or familiar with you. Students should never call teachers by their first names or nicknames.**
    There is a difference between being "friendly" and being "friends" with students. Boundaries between adults and young persons must be enforced. Insisting on proper titles is one way to keep boundaries.

3. **Do not engage in private correspondence with students. If you receive personal communication from a student**

**and the communication is not appropriate, keep a copy
of the communication and do not respond unless you
have received permission from a supervisor.**

It is common for students to develop "crushes" on teachers, to
fantasize about them, and/or to try to communicate on a peer level. If
one receives student letters, etc. that are romantic, sexual, or otherwise
inappropriate, it is best not to respond and to report the occurrence to
one's supervisor for everyone's protection.

4. **Do not visit students in their homes unless their parents are present.**

Being alone with young persons can give an appearance of impropriety. Many instances of sexual abuse are alleged to have occurred
when adults were present in students home when the parents were absent. In particular, if there is no one home but the student, the situation can quickly become your word against the student's.

5. **Do not invite students to your home.**

The comments pertaining to guideline four also apply here.

6. **Do not transport students in your vehicle.**

Obviously, there exists the same problematic situation of an
adult being alone with a student or students. Additionally, the adult
may assume personal liability for any accident or injury. It can be very
tempting to respond to a student's request for a ride home, but a better approach would be to wait in an open area with the student until
transportation arrives or to direct the student to an administrator.

7. **Do not take the role of surrogate parent with a student.**

Educators are not the parents of their students and do not have
the responsibilities or privileges of parents. While being supportive
and helpful, educators must respect the rights of parents. Some parents, feeling teachers have displaced them in their children's affections,
are seeking restraining orders against the educators.

8. **Do not criticize a student's parents to the student.**

No matter how poorly the parents behave, they are most likely the only parents their children will have. If you believe a child is abused or neglected, contact the appropriate authorities.

9. Do not give students your cell phone number without the permission and knowledge of your supervisor.

Communicating with students via cell phone on a regular basis can give an appearance, even if not the reality, of impropriety. It is best to call students from the school or parish phones if possible.

10. Do not communicate with students from your home e-mail address.

E-mail was the topic of the November, 2003 NCEA Notes article by this author and readers may want to refer to it. In brief, communicating with students from home e-mail addresses can give an appearance of secrecy. Educators should always use their school or parish e-mail accounts.

Do not hire students to work in your home without the express knowledge and consent of your supervisor. Mixing roles is generally not a good idea. Acting as a young person's employer while serving as teacher can "muddy" the waters where boundaries are concerned. For example, a male teacher taking a babysitter home at midnight is placing himself in a particularly vulnerable position should the student make a claim of inappropriate conduct. Additionally, teachers can incur liability for injuries students sustain while in their employment.

11. A good premise is to ask, "How would I feel if what I am doing were to appear on the front page of the paper tomorrow?"

Many problems could be avoided if adults would ask themselves this question before certain interactions with young people. An even better question might be, "Would Jesus do this?" Fidelity to prayer and the exercise of common sense can help educators avoid boundary "pitfalls" and can protect everyone.

FOR REFLECTION AND DISCUSSION

- The fifteen students in your Advanced Placement class have all scored '5' on the AP exam. This is the first time in the history of the school that anything like this has happened. You asked the principal if an assembly could be held to recognize the students' achievement, but he said "no" as there were already "too many things scheduled." One of the students, Mary Lou, brought a note from her mother saying that she and her husband think the students are entitled to a nice celebration. She is offering their large home, pool and yard for swimming and a barbecue (no alcohol, of course) the following Sunday. She wants you to know that she and her husband will be visiting his mother in another state that day but their 20 year old, "very responsible" daughter will be at home and is willing to supervise. Plus, she adds, you will be there, so nothing could go wrong. You want the students to have a nice celebration but you are not particularly comfortable with what is being proposed. You could bring another adult with you, but you are not sure that you should accept the invitation and the responsibility. How will you respond to Mary Lou's mother and to the students who are excited about the proposed celebration?

Chapter Nine

KEEPING STUDENT CONFIDENCES: WHAT CAN YOU TELL? WHAT MUST YOU TELL?

ONE OF THE MORE perplexing situations facing Catholic educators today is that presented by student sharing of confidential information. Today's young persons may well face more pressures and problems than young persons of any other decade. Broken homes, alcoholism and drug addiction, sexual and physical abuse, depression, and violence were certainly found in earlier eras, but they seem to be more prevalent, or at least more openly acknowledged, than they were 20 or 30 years ago. The responsibility for receiving student confidences and advising students in both day-to-day situations and crises can be overwhelming. Busy teachers may ask, "What am I supposed to do? I'm not a professional counselor, a psychiatrist, or a social worker but I'm the one the student trusts, the one the student has consulted." Are there certain legal issues involved in receiving student confidences? Are there matters that must be made known to others, even when the student has asked for and received a promise of confidentiality?

These are good questions for any educator to ask. Teachers cannot afford to think that they can help all students all the time. It is not possible. If a student were to come to a teacher and tell the teacher he or she is experiencing shortness of breath and chest pain, the teacher would quickly summon both the student's parents and medical assistance. Yet, psychological problems are no less serious than physical ones, and the layperson that attempts to deal with such problems un-aided may well be courting tragedy for both self and student.

Confidentiality

Confidentiality is generally held to mean that one individual or individuals will keep private information that has been given to them, and will not reveal it. For example, the person who receives the sacrament of reconciliation rightfully expects that the subject matter of confession will be held sacred by the confessor and will not be revealed to anyone. Indeed, there are accounts of priests who died rather than break the seal of confession.

Friends share confidences with each other. One individual may say to another, "This is confidential. You cannot repeat it." The person speaking in confidence has a right to expect that the confidant to whom the information has been given will keep the matter confidential. But there are recognized limits to what friends will keep confidential. If one's friend confides that she has been stockpiling sleeping medication and plans to take all of it that evening so as to commit suicide, it is not hard to see that morality demands that the confidant communicate that knowledge to a spouse or other family member of the confiding individual, or take some other action that would intervene in the attempted suicide.

It is not unheard of for teachers to believe that students who talk about suicide are not serious, or can be talked out of the planned action, or are not capable of carrying out a threatened suicide. As child and adolescent psychologists report, young people do not think through the long-term ramifications of a suicide attempt. There is also, among some young people, a fascination with death as can be seen by the idolization of famous people who have died young or committed suicide.

If a student tells a teacher that he or she is going to harm self or others, the teacher must reveal that information even if a promise of confidentiality has been given. In a number of lawsuits brought against teachers and school districts, parents sought damages from teachers who were told by students in confidence that they planned to harm themselves or others; the teachers did not contact parents or other authorities. In some cases, the educators were held to be negligent by failing to warn.

Legal Immunity

It is a widely held myth that counselors, physicians, psychologists, and social workers have legal immunity from responsibility for any injuries that may arise from their not acting on confidential information presented to them. Counselors and teachers have no immunity and must reveal what they know if someone's life or health is at risk. A counselor who hears from a young person that the individual plans to kill his or her parents and does nothing about it will not be legally able to decline to answer questions under oath nor will the counselor be held harmless for any resulting injuries if he or she decides not to revel the threats. Counselors and teachers must make it very clear to confiding individuals that they will keep their confidences unless their health, life or safety or those of another are involved.

The only two privileges from disclosure of confidentiality information remaining in the majority of states are that of priest/penitent and attorney/client. Even the husband/wife privilege, which allowed a spouse to refuse to testify against a spouse, has been largely abandoned.

In light of the above facts, a teacher must presume that no legal protection exists for those who receive student confidences. What should the teacher who wants to be a role model for young persons--who want to be approachable and helpful, do? The answer is simple: lay down the ground rules for confidentiality before you receive any confidences. Tell students you will respect their confidences except in cases of life, health and safety. If a student asks to talk to you in confidence, reiterate the ground rules before the student begins to share.

Journal Writing

Religion, language arts, English, psychology and other subject matter teachers have long recognized the value of student journal writing. This practice does, however, carry a real risk of student disclosure of information that the teacher is compelled to reveal. Teachers must set the rules for confidentiality.

Teachers must understand that they are expected to read what students write. If a teacher cannot read the assignment, then the assignment should not be given. In particular, teachers should avoid such techniques as telling students to clip together pages they do not wish the teacher to read or to write at the top of such pages, "Please do not read." Journal writing has a place in today's curriculum, but teachers must be sure that students understand the parameters of the assignment and of the teacher's responsibilities for reporting threatened danger.

Retreats

The retreat experience is extremely important for today's Catholic young people. However, students are often at their most vulnerable in such situations. They may share stories of child abuse, sexual harassment, family dysfunction, and even possible criminal activity. While encouraging students to share, the group leader must once again set the ground rules before the sharing beings. The use of peer leaders does not lessen the responsibility of the supervising adults. Student leaders must be told of the ground rules and of the necessity to communicate them to group members as well as procedures to be followed in notifying adults if matter is revealed in sessions that must be reported.

Case law

In one case, *Brooks v. Logan and Joint District No. 2* (1995), heard by the Idaho Court of Appeals, parents of a student who had committed suicide filed an action for wrongful death and a claim for negligent infliction of emotional distress against a teacher who had assigned the keeping of journals to her class. Jeff Brooks was a student at Meridian High School and was assigned to Ms. Logan's English class. Students were asked to make entries into a daily journal as part of their English composition work. For a period of four months prior to his death, Jeff wrote in his journal.

After his death, Ms. Logan read through the entries and gave the journal to a school counselor, who delivered it to Jeff's parents. Jeff had made journal entries that indicated that he was depressed and that he was contemplating suicide. One entry read as follows:

> Well, Edgar Allen Poe, I can live with studying about that stuff he wrote especially the one short story about the evil eye. . . . I used to write poems until I pronounced myself dead in one of them and how could I write poems or stories if I was dead. . . .

Recently . . . see I went into a medium depression and wrote poems to two special people. . . . I told them it was too bad that
I had to say goodbye this way like that but, it would be the
only way and I felt better. . . . (903 Pac. Rptr. 2nd, p. 81).

Ms. Logan maintained that Jeff had requested that she not
read his entries, so that he would feel free to express himself. The journal contained a note in which Ms. Logan stated that she would not read
the journal for content, but would only check for dates and length.
The parents maintained that, in a conversation with Ms. Logan after
their receipt of the journal, she stated that she had "reread the entries."
Ms Logan denied that she made that statement, and contends that she
did not read the entries in question until after Jeff's death.

The lower court granted summary judgment in favor of the teacher and the school district. However, the appellate court reversed the
finding, and held that there were issues of fact in existence which
could only be determined at trial. Thus, a trial court was charged
with determining whether Ms. Logan's actions or inactions constituted
negligence contributing to Jeff's death. Part of the analysis includes
a determination as to whether Jeff's suicide was foreseeable: would a
reasonable person in Ms, Logan's place have recognized the possibility
of suicide and notified someone? The appellate court refers to similar
case law in which jailers have been held liable for the suicide of prisoners when the prisoners had exhibited warning signs.

This case and the discussion indicate the vulnerability of teachers who receive student confidences. The wise Catholic educator
will establish and enforce ground rules for dealing with student confidences, and will seek help from school officials and/or *parents when
appropriate.*

FOR REFLECTION AND DISCUSSION

- Do your students know what your rules are concerning keeping student confidences? If your principal asks you to explain those rules, how would you respond?
- Student D asks to see you after school. She says that her friend, Student E, is pregnant and planning to terminate her pregnancy. E has not told her parents but D & E both think E's parents will force her to have an abortion, even if she objects. What will you do?

Chapter Ten

CHILD ABUSE AND NEGLECT

THE NUMBERS OF CHILD ABUSE and neglect reports have risen at an alarming rate in the last decade. The media carry daily reports of adults causing children physical and emotional pain. The educator is in a particularly sensitive position. Adolescents often choose teachers as confidantes in their struggles to deal with abuse and its effects. For this reason, principals must ensure that teachers and all school employees are as prepared as possible to deal with the realities of abuse and neglect. Principals would be well advised to spend some time reviewing pertinent state law and school policies and providing at least a few minutes of discussion on the topic at one of the first faculty meetings of the year. If a separate meeting is not provided for other school employees such as secretaries, custodians and cafeteria workers, the principal should consider having them present for the appropriate portion of the faculty meeting.

Statutory considerations

All fifty states have laws requiring educators to report suspected abuse and/or neglect. A decade ago, the vast majority of states designated certain professionals, such as teachers and physicians, as mandated reporters. Today, an increasing number of states has dropped the list of mandated reports in favor of requiring "any adult" to make a report.

Statutes generally mandate reporting procedures. The reporting individual usually makes a phone report that is followed by a written report within a specified period, often 48 hours, although some states have different procedures. Statutes usually provide protection for a person who makes a good-faith report of child abuse that later is discovered to be unfounded. Such a good-faith reporter will not be liable to the alleged abuser for defamation of character. However, a person can be held liable for making what is referred to as a "malicious report," one which has no basis in fact and which was made by a person who knows that no factual basis existed. Conversely, statutes usually mandate that a person who knew of child abuse or neglect and failed to report it can be fined and/or charged with a misdemeanor or felony.

Defining Abuse

What is child abuse? This author once heard an attorney define it as "corporal punishment gone too far." Although it excludes sexual abuse, the definition has merit. It poses these questions: How far is too far? Who makes the final determination? Are there any allowances for differing cultural practices? It is difficult, if not impossible, to give a precise definition that will cover all eventualities. Certainly, some situations are so extreme that there can be little argument that abuse has occurred. A student who appears at school with cigarette burns has been abused, even if the abuse is self-inflicted. When a child alleges sexual abuse, there exist only three conclusions: first, the child is telling the truth, second, the child is somehow mistaken about what has occurred, and third, the child is lying. The investigating agency will have to determine which conclusion is correct.

The majority of cases will probably not be clear-cut and an educator may well struggle to decide if a report should be made. Many law enforcement officials and some attorneys instruct educators to report everything that students tell them that could possibly constitute abuse or negligence. They further caution teachers that it is not their job to determine if abuse has occurred. As a child abuse reporter, the teacher's function is to present the information. Appropriate officials will determine whether the report should be investigated further or simply "screened out" as a well-intentioned report that does not appear to be in the category of abuse.

In-Service Education

School administrators should provide teachers, other employees and volunteers with some in-service training indicators of child abuse and neglect, and the legal procedures for reporting such conditions.

There are many excellent written resources available. Local police departments and social service agencies are usually happy to make both materials and speakers available to schools. If a school does not provide its teachers with education and materials on this topic, a phone call to appropriate sources should provide the teacher with needed materials.

Filing a Report

The obligation to report belongs to the person with the suspicion and cannot be handed on to another. When the first edition of this text appeared, school and/or diocesan policy may have required that a teacher report suspected child abuse to the principal who would then make the report. Such a policy no longer meets the requirements of the law. If a staff member files a report, the principal should be notified that a report has been made. It is legally dangerous for the school when a police officer or other official appears to investigate a report of child abuse, and the principal does not know that a report has been filed.

Schools officials should decide in advance how visits and requests from police or social workers will be handled. Many states require that school personnel allow officials to examine and question students. Principals should seek legal counsel in determining the applicable law for a given state. If the law permits the examination and questioning of a child, a school official should ask to be present if the student is comfortable with the school employee being present. In some jurisdictions, the investigating official may refuse to allow school personnel to be present.

Teachers and Abuse

A survey of educational cases decided in courts of record reveals that the number of lawsuits alleging teacher or other school employee abuse of children is increasing. While administrators can be found responsible for the acts of subordinates, courts appear unwilling to hold administrators liable for an employee's abuse of students unless there is clear evidence of administrative misconduct. Two cases are particularly illustrative. In the 1990 case of *Medlin v. Bass*, school officials were found innocent of misconduct in their supervision of an educator guilty of abuse. The North Carolina Court of Appeals held that the abuser's crime was outside the scope of employment and there were no compelling reasons for his superiors to investigate his background more thoroughly than they did. In *D. T. et al. v. Ind. School District No. 16 of Pawnee County*, the United States Court of Appeals, Tenth Circuit, declined to hold school officials responsible for teacher abuse of students occurring during a summer fund raising campaign. A particularly troubling aspect of this case was the fact that the teacher had a previous conviction for sodomy. The decision notwithstanding, today it is more likely that a principal would be held liable if a reasonable record check or criminal check would have revealed that a potential employee had a criminal record involving child abuse. Additionally, failing to perform background checks is a violation of the laws of most states. It is well established that schools can attract persons with abusive tendencies who seek children upon whom to prey. Thus, it is important that school officials do everything in their power to investigate the background of persons before employment.

The vast majority of states now mandate that persons who work with children be fingerprinted. Each applicant must also sign an authorization of a police check of his or her name for any criminal arrests and/ or convictions. Conviction of a crime is not an automatic or permanent bar to employment. Many states prohibit persons who have been convicted of violent or sexual crimes from working with young persons. On employment applications, administrators may wish to include a statement such as: "Conviction of a crime is not an automatic bar to employment. Please provide all pertinent details. Decisions will be made as required by law."

Any student or parent complaint alleging child abuse by a teacher must be taken seriously. Failure to do so can put the school and its officials at grave legal risk. Administrators and school boards should adopt policies governing reporting child abuse/neglect by staff before the need for such policies surfaces. It is preferable to have a policy that is never needed then to have no policy and be forced to try to construct one when faced with a need.

For Reflection and Discussion

- If asked, how would you define child abuse?
- Student Z, whom you taught last year, asked to see you. She tells you that she has been tied to a chair in a dark, unheated closet and her father pours water from a pitcher on her head. She is left there in freezing weather. She asks you to turn her father in to the authorities so that he will get off her back. What will you do?
- You have a very uneasy feeling about the teacher whose classroom is next to yours. He often has one female student alone in his classroom with him for an hour or two after school. You have heard whispered conversation among students, but as soon as you appear interested, the students stop talking. Today, you noticed that he has placed dark construction paper over the window in his classroom door. You knocked on the door, attempted to turn the doorknob, and found the door locked. A half hour later, you observed a girl leaving his classroom. She was buttoning her blouse and pulling down her skirt. You started to call her into your room, but decided against it. However, you know you must do something. What will you do?

Chapter Eleven

SEXUAL HARRASSMENT: WHAT IS IT? WHAT DOES IT MEAN FOR THE CATHOLIC SCHOOL TEACHER?

SEXUAL HARASSMENT HAS BECOME a common term in the last decade or so. Newspapers carry stories of alleged sexual harassment and resulting lawsuits. No longer is sexual harassment something that is found only between two adults or between an adult and a child. School children claim that peers have harassed them. The news stories can seem overwhelming, and the potential for legal liability great. What, then, can the Catholic schoolteacher do?

Administrators and teachers should first ensure that they understand what sexual harassment is. Every comment that is made concerning gender is not sexual harassment. For example, a male student who states, "Everyone knows boys are better at math than girls," or a teacher who declares, "I'd rather teach girls since they are not as rowdy as boys," is not necessarily guilty of sexual harassment. Title VII of the Civil Rights Act of 1964 mandated that the workplace be free of harassment based on sex. Title IX requires that educational programs receiving federal funding be free of sexual harassment. Both these titled laws are anti-discrimination statutes.

Federal anti-discrimination law can bind Catholic institutions. Most schools now file statements of compliance with discrimination laws with appropriate local, state and national authorities. Anti-discrimination legislation can impact Catholic schools because the government has a compelling interest in the equal treatment of all citizens. Compliance with statutory law can be required if there is no less burdensome way to meet the requirements of the law. Regardless of the applicability of the law, fairness requires that schools strive to be fair in the administration of all programs.

Many government agencies, most notably the Equal Employment Opportunities Commission, issued definitions of forbidden sexual harassment. These definitions include unwelcome sexual advances or comments, requests for sexual behaviors, and other sexual verbal or physical conduct when:

- An individual's performance of such acts is a condition of employment or academic requirements
- Performance of such conduct is made explicitly or implicitly a term of employment
- Submission to, or rejection of such conduct is used as the basis for an employment or academic decision
- Such conduct has the intention or effect of interfering with an individual's work or academic performance, or creates a hostile or intimidating environment.

Courts, including the U.S, Supreme Court, are vigorously supporting persons' rights to be free from sexual harassment.

In the 1992 case of *Franklin v. Gwinnet County Public Schools*, the United States Supreme Court ruled that monetary damages can be awarded students whose rights under Title IX have been violated. In this case a teacher had allegedly sexually harassed a student for several years. The harassment consisted of conversations, kissing, telephone calls, and forced sexual relations. The school system maintained that no relief could be given the student since Title IX remedies had been limited to back pay and employment relief. The court disagreed, held that students who suffer harassment are entitled to damages, and remanded the case to the lower court for a determination of damages. Although this is not a recent case, it was one of the first to reach the United States Supreme Court and remains a groundbreaking case. Thus, it would appear that if Title IX applies to the Catholic school, students are protected against sexual harassment in much the same manner that employees are protected.

Harassment Actions

The following are examples of behaviors that could constitute sexual harassment: sexual propositions, suggestive jokes, inappropriate physical contact, innuendos, sexual offers, looks, and gestures. In a number of public school cases, female students alleged that male students made sexual statements to them and that school officials, after being informed, declined to take action and stated "boys will be boys." Many of these cases have been settled out of court and money has been paid to the alleged victims.

Although one can argue that the person who sexually harasses another should be liable and not the school and its administrators, case law is suggesting that administrators who ignore such behavior or do not take it seriously can be held liable to the offended parties. (For another example please consult the 1990 case, *Jane Doe v. Special Sch. Dist. of St Louis County.*)

Suggested Policies

One of the most important actions an administrator can take with regard to sexual harassment is to develop clear policies defining sexual harassment and detailing procedures for dealing with claims that sexual harassment has occurred. Teachers and other staff members are required to implement the policies. The following is one suggestion of a policy statement.

Sexual harassment is defined as:

1. Threatening to impose adverse employment, academic or disciplinary or other sanctions on a person, unless favors are given; and/or
2. Conduct, containing sexual matter or suggestions that would be offensive to a reasonable person.

Sexual harassment includes, but is not limited to, the following behaviors:

1. Verbal conduct such as epithets, derogatory jokes or comments, slurs or unwanted sexual advances, imitations, or comments;
2. Visual contact such as derogatory and/or sexually oriented posters, photography, cartoons, drawings, or gestures;

3. Physical contact such as assault, unwanted touching, block-ing normal movements, or interfering with work, study, or play because of sex;
4. Threats and demands to submit to sexual requests as a con-dition of continued employment or grades or other benefits, or to avoid some other loss and offers of benefits in return for sexual favors; and
5. Retaliation for having reported or threatened to report sex-ual harassment.

Procedures for reporting should then be given. These proce-dures should include a statement such as, "All allegations will be tak-en seriously and promptly investigated." Confidentiality should be stressed. Concern should be expressed for both the alleged victim and the alleged perpetrator. Any forms that are to be used should be in-cluded in the procedures.

Every employee should be required to sign a statement that he or she has been given a copy of the policies relating to sexual harassment and other sexual misconduct, has read the material, and agrees to be bound by it. Parent/student handbooks should contain at least a gen-eral statement that sexual harassment is not condoned in a Christian atmosphere, and both parents and students should sign a statement that they agree to be governed by the handbook.

Prevention

It is far easier to prevent claims of sexual harassment than it is to defend them. To that end, teachers and other employees should par-ticipate in appropriate in-service training that raises awareness of sexual harassment and other gender issues. Staff members must understand what sorts of behaviors can be construed as sexual harassment.

Teachers should discuss issues of fair treatment of oth-ers with their students, and should promptly correct any students who demean others. Defenses such as, "I was only kidding," will not be accepted if the alleged victim states that the behavior was offensive and unwelcome, and a court finds that a reasonable per-son could find the behavior offensive and unwelcome. Finally, sexual harassment and other forms of demeaning behavior have no place in a Catholic school. Guarding the dignity of each member of the school community should be a priority for all Catholic educators.

FOR REFLECTION AND DISCUSSION

- Can you define sexual harassment if asked to do so by a parent or student?
- How would you handle the following scenario? You are supervising a student mixer. You see a thirteen-year-old girl sitting by the bathroom and weeping. You ask what is wrong. She gives you the name of a male student and says, 'He told me my cup size has to be bigger than my head. I'm afraid to go back on the dance floor. Am I really so big?"
- How would you respond to faculty room conversation that seems to center around one female staff member and the "revealing" clothes she wears? You notice that both male and female teachers are now participating in a rating system and taking bets as to how revealing (on a scale of 1-10) her clothes will be the next day. You have also heard comments about how she must be unfaithful to her husband. No one has actually said anything to her face, but you cannot imagine that she is unaware of what is being said about her. What is your responsibility in this situation? How will you meet that responsibility?

Chapter Twelve

Students With Special Needs in Catholic Schools: What Is the Catholic Educator's Responsibility?

MENTION THE TOPIC OF STUDENTS with special needs who are seeking admission and/or retention in Catholic schools and comments will run the gamut including: Catholic schools are not equipped for such kids; special needs students can go to the public schools where they will get the services they need; teachers are not prepared to teach special needs students and do not want to learn how to teach them; special needs students don't fit in; it is not Catholic schools' responsibility; in the past, there were fifty kids in a classroom, everybody learned, and nobody talked about special needs. Until the 1970s, Catholic and other private schools could do whatever they liked in regard to accepting or not accepting students with special needs. There is an old adage that a person can do whatever he or she wants until somebody challenges you, takes you to the court, and the judge says you can't do it. For decades, Catholic school handbooks and admissions materials maintained policies that stated their schools were not equipped for students with special needs and that they could not admit such students. Although such policies are illegal since the 1970s, reports suggest that some Catholic schools continue to maintain such policies today.

Section 504 of the Rehabilitation Act of 1973 and the 1992

Americans with Disabilities Act can seem like a legal quagmire for the educator. Myths and half-truths abound. Some consultants and lawyers advise that schools must be made totally accessible. Many administrators fear that the cost of accommodations will be so high as to force schools out of existence. Other administrators question the appropriateness of accepting students with special needs in college preparatory schools. Can the average Catholic school provide the proper program adjustments needed by these students? Catholic school personnel need a clear understanding of legal requirements.

Discrimination Law

Federal law prohibits discrimination on the basis of race, sex, disability, age and national origin. Although discrimination on the basis of religion or creed is also prohibited, the right of religious institutions to give preference to their own members is upheld. This means that Catholic schools may give preference to Catholic students and may give hiring preference to Catholic teachers and other employees. Religious preference is legal, even if the person(s) excluded in the exercise of the preference belong to another protected class, such as race, sex, national origin or disability, so long as the exclusion is not based on a classification other than religion.

Public Law 94- 142 and Successor Laws

Catholic school administrators must understand the law governing students with special needs. Public law 94-142, the Education of All Handicapped Children Act, and its successor laws, including the Individuals with Disabilities in Education Act and No Child Left Behind mandate a free and appropriate education for all children. There is no requirement that Catholic schools provide "free and appropriate education;" however, the state may place a child in a private school if that placement seems to provide the most appropriate education. In such a case, the state would be responsible for the tuition.

Catholic schools are not required to meet every need of every child. Most private schools are not equipped to offer educational services to everyone. The fact that a school does not have to offer services does not mean that a student attending that school has no right to such services. The law gives all students rights. A private school student has a right to request and receive from the public school an evaluation and, if necessary, an individual educational plan (IEP). The public school must make every reasonable effort to provide the student with services needed even if the student remains in the private school. If it is not practical to offer such services to a private school student, the public school officials can draw up an IEP that calls for public school education. A parent is always free to accept or reject such an IEP. If a parent elects to keep a child in a private school over the objections of professional educators working with that child, the public school cannot be held responsible for the child's progress nor can the public school be required to pay private school tuition.

It is important to note that the private school student and the public school student have the same federal protections. The private school student is entitled to the same services a public school student is entitled to receive; however, the private school student may not be able to insist that the services be provided within a private school as part of an IEP.

Standards of Supervision

Principals, many of whom are familiar with the adage, "the younger the child chronologically or mentally, the greater the standard of care," may ask, "If we accept students with special needs, are we committing ourselves to higher levels of supervision?" Teachers can be held to different standards. For example, a teacher who is supervising a senior honors class will probably be held to a lower standard that would an individual teaching kindergarten children. Courts assume that older children can be expected to take some responsibility for themselves.

Mental age is concerned with the effect that a disability may have on a child. If a Catholic school accepts a student with a mental disability, teachers must accommodate the disability. If a child performs well below grade level and exhibits immature behavior, a teacher may be expected to provide more stringent supervision than that given to other students. Not all disabilities are mental, nor are they permanent. If a child is an amputee, the child will need more supervision and help in physical activities than others may need.

Discipline

All students need to be accountable to persons in authority. Special needs children are no exception. Schools have the right to require that all students abide by codes of conduct. Every student in a Catholic school should be expected to obey the rules.

Exceptions are in order only when the infraction is the result of the disability. If students who use walkers or crutches cannot get to class on time because they simply cannot move fast enough, it would be unfair to penalize them for being late. Another example is presented by a student with Tourette's syndrome, which is often characterized by bizarre behavior such as swearing. If a student suffering from Tourette's were to use profanity, it might be unfair to discipline the student if the behavior is beyond the student's control.

What the Law Requires

The Disability Law of 1973 requires that otherwise qualified persons with disabilities be offered reasonable accommodations, those that an institution could be expected to fund. It would not be reasonable to suppose that a Catholic school should institute a special program, with special education teachers, for a blind student or a profoundly mentally handicapped student.

Disability laws require that institutions not discriminate against persons who are seeking admission to their programs. If a disabled person can participate in the program with a reasonable amount of accommodation, then the institution must provide the accommodation. If providing that support system would create a significant hardship, the institution will not have to provide it. For example, if a blind student sought admission and acceptance to a school, the school would need to hire a special teacher or aide for the student . The school would probably not be expected to incur those expenses.

Another significant issue is accessibility of all members of the public, at least those with a legitimate reason, to be present at the school. Disabled parents have moral and ethical rights, as well as legal rights, to attend functions in which their children participate and to attend parent events, such as parent/ teacher conferences. Regardless of the requirements of disability law, Gospel imperatives in addition to the doctrine of fairness, require that educators make every reasonable effort to accommodate special needs students. Reasonable effort does not usually mean spending hundreds of thousands of dollars to install elevators, but it may mean moving the parent / teacher conferences to a more accessible location, such as a gym.

Because one is not *legally* required to do something does not mean that one should not do that thing, if it is the right thing to do. If a school has enough assets to afford a sign language interpreter for a deaf student, or instructions in signing for the faculty and staff, the educator may have a moral and ethical duty to provide for the student even though the law does not require such provision. Indeed, the Pastoral Statement of U.S. Catholic Bishops on Handicapped People (1978) seems to demand such action: "If handicapped people are to become equal partners in the Christian community, injustices must be eliminated." Certainly, Catholic schools should be leaders in fighting injustice wherever it is found, especially as it affects those whose disabilities place them among those for whom Christ manifested special concern.

The Right to the Best Education

All students have the right to a free and appropriate education according to federal law. Students must be evaluated for special services at parental request, but the law does not entitle students to a special needs program. Catholic school students have the same right to evaluation, as do public school students. However, the program recommended as a result of the evaluation may not be available in the Catholic school, which is only required to make reasonable accommodations.

FOR REFLECTION AND DISCUSSION

- A student with diagnosed learning disorders tells you that he will be taping your classes from now on "because the doctor said it would help." How do you respond?
- The principal has brought a "problem" case to the faculty for advice. Mrs. K, who already has two children in your school and one who has graduated, has asked the school to admit her daughter who is totally blind. She says it will be no problem for the school to have materials translated into Braille and that student helpers can be assigned to her daughter to assist her in getting around the building. Do you think the school should accept this student? Why or why not? What legal issues do you see?
- The principal has admitted a student who has a diagnosis of severe Asperger's Syndrome, coupled with extreme sensitivity to stimuli. This student will be in your class. The principal's memo states that accommodations include: allowing the student to stand, rather than sit, whenever he wishes; allowing the student to be the first or last one in and out of the classroom; giving a copy of your notes— or having a student make a copy of his or her notes—to the student everyday a daily note to parents about progress; and fewer test items on every test. How will you respond?

Chapter Thirteen

EXTRA-CURRICULAR
ACTIVITIES

EXTRA-CURRICULAR ACTIVITIES HAVE LONG been a part of secondary education. Such activities include, but are not limited to speech and debate clubs, athletic games/intramurals, and choir recitals, to name a few. With these activities comes an increased concern for legal issues.

An administrator may notice some problems with activities and promise that next year will be different. Teachers who sponsor extra-curricular activities will understand their various responsibilities and will conscientiously perform their duties. Academic and behavioral requirements for extra-curricular participation will be published and enforced. Some plan for dealing with students who are dropped off for practices or activities well before an adult supervisor is present or who are still present on campus long after activities will be in place. However, as any seasoned educator knows, next year comes all too soon.

Faculty and staff should be involved in the development of a plan for improvement of the programs offered. Staff members should be encouraged to submit their suggestions for improvement in writing. Thus, as the season closes, the administrator and moderator can meet to determine policies and procedures for the coming year.

Extra-curricular and co-curricular activities are, by their very nature, more dangerous than ordinary classroom activities. Participants and their parents can appear to care far more passionately about extra-curricular programs than about curriculum offerings. An angry student or parent can always threaten a lawsuit. The reasonable educator will not be unduly alarmed when threats are made; if policies and procedures are properly developed and implemented, the administrator will be in the best possible position.

Assigning and Training Moderators

The assignment and the replacement of moderators during the year can present critical challenges for the administrator. There is a great temptation to take anyone who expresses interest in the activity and make that person the moderator. Such a procedure is particularly dangerous in athletics, which will be discussed in greater detail in the next chapter. While a person does not need to be an expert wrestler to coach wrestling or an outstanding actor to direct the play, the individual should be willing to study the requirements for coaching a team or directing a play. At the same time, persons who played a sport or acted in a play may believe that they can direct the activity when, in fact, previous participation does not ensure the ability to teach another the skill. Administrators must ensure that persons who moderate activities possess at least minimum understanding of the activity. For example, released time, or other incentives, can be provided to allow a neophyte moderator to visit a more experienced one or to choose a mentor at another school. Such actions may be time-consuming, but they provide the best protection for the safety of students and the best defense against liability in the case of injury.

The applicant's experience and qualifications to serve as a moderator must be verified. If one has no actual experience participating in the activity, one should be able to indicate how one has or will acquire the necessary knowledge or skills. If the moderator appears to be truly inexperienced and untried, that individual should not be assigned complete responsibility for the students participating the activity. The individual, however, could be assigned as an assistant to a more experienced faculty member. Some activities do not require the same level of previous experience as others. A teacher who did not belong to the National Honor Society in high school may still moderate the society. However, an individual who has never acted in a play, participated in stage or set crews, has trouble keeping order, and states that she has no interest in drama and thinks it is a waste of time, should not be assigned to moderate the drama club.

Secondary school educators may ask whether using a volunteer as a moderator is advisable. There are certainly times and occasions when such an action may be best. If someone's mother had extensive experience in college musicals, she may be able to direct the school play; she may even be more qualified to do so than anyone on the faculty. A student's father who was a football captain may be able to serve as an outstanding coach. While the use of volunteers is legally acceptable, the principal or other administrator must ensure that the individual is a person of integrity and trustworthiness. Criminal background checks must be done. References should be requested and checked so that individuals with pedophile tendencies and charming personalities are not inadvertently assigned to positions of great trust. While no one can avert every possible tragedy, the wise administrator will follow diocesan procedure and have other procedures in place to gather the necessary background information concerning volunteers.

Diocesan and/or local administrators should consider an annual orientation for extracurricular moderators. Athletic coaches may be offered a separate orientation. In the unfortunate event of an injury, educational administrators could demonstrate that they had taken their responsibilities seriously and had tried to ensure that moderators and coaches were competent.

Student Selection and Standards for Participation

Most administrators have heard parent and/or student complaints regarding non-selection for an activity. Administrators should insist that moderators and coaches develop, publish, and implement clear standards for selection. Obviously, selection can be a subjective process. The drama moderator may strongly believe that a 300-pound female student will not make a believable Maria in the Sound of Music even if she has an outstanding singing voice. Another moderator may decide that voice quality is more important than appearance. Feelings do get hurt. The administrator who insists on clear standards and monitors the performance of moderators and coaches can be satisfied that the requirements of fairness are met. The administrator should guard against taking the side of a parent or student in a dispute over selection for, or retention in, an activity unless the moderator/ coach is clearly in the wrong. One of the worst situations for a moderator and administrator to be in is one in which the administrator "second guesses" the decisions of the moderator.

Non-selection for a part or position one really wanted presents an opportunity for life lessons. No one always gets what he or she wants. Life does not always appear to be fair. When the author was a high school principal, the mother of one of the students who did not get the lead in the play came to complain to her. Realizing that the author was not going to overturn the director's decision, the lady stated, "I hope you know that this is the worst thing that has ever happened or ever will happen to my daughter." The author replied, "If this is the worst thing that ever happens to your daughter, what a blessed life she will have. You are her mother. Please help her understand that." Educators should not just be concerned with legalities, but also with the realities of life in a competitive world.

Each activity and each moderator will have some rules and regulations to which the student participant must adhere. Some may be general school rules. Others may be specific to the activity. Further, in the case of athletics and drama, for example, state associations may provide other standards. Rules and regulations should be standardized as far as possible. It seems very unfair for an athlete with a failing grade to be "benched," while another student with a similar grade is allowed to sing the lead in the school play. Everyone who participates in extra-curricular activities should abide by some common code of conduct.

Some rules and regulations that might be considered could include:

- Attendance during the school day in order to participate in an activity;
- Academic requirements (minimum grade averages, for example) for participation;
- Behavior requirements (a student who is suspended from school should not participate in an extra-curricular activity)

Administrative Monitoring

School administrators need to be familiar with the rules and regulations of every activity in their schools. Certainly, they cannot be expected to recall every rule at any given moment, but they should have access to every rule and be able to obtain it if they cannot summon it from memory.

Key administrators need to be physically present at athletic events and other extra-curricular activities. No principal should be expected to be at every game or activity, but administrators should ensure that there is some administrative supervision throughout the course of the year. Some state athletic associations require that an administrator be present at every interscholastic game. Regular meetings with moderators and coaches can also keep everyone informed and help to minimize problems.

For Reflection and Discussion

- Your principal has asked you to become the moderator of the fencing club. You have never fenced in your life. Your principal states that all you have to do is be present at practices and games; he/she insists that you don't need to know anything about fencing. How will you respond?
- The parents of Student Q have just come to your classroom without an appointment. Q did not get a major role in the school play you direct. The parents state that last year's director (who has moved to another school) promised that Q would get a big part if Q took acting lessons from him at the rate of $50 an hour. The parents want Q to have a major part, or in the alternative, a refund of the $2,000 spent on acting lessons. What will you say and/or do?
- Your best friend's daughter, who is also your godchild, is trying out for a position/role, etc. in an activity you moderate. She is good, but so are other students. You are afraid that should you choose her, you will be accused of favoritism. Your friend recently said to you, "Remember, just because she is your godchild, she shouldn't be made to meet a higher standard. Don't choose someone less qualified just because you don't want to look prejudiced." As your friend turned to walk away, he/she added, "We've been friends for decades. I'd hate to end this friendship because you don't choose her." Clearly, you are between the proverbial "rock and a hard place." What will you do?

Chapter Fourteen

LEGAL CONCERNS REGARDING ATHLETICS

ATHLETICS, LIKE ALL EXTRA-CURRICULAR ACTIVITIES, pose some of the greatest legal concerns for schools, and programs in Catholic schools are no exception. Principals, athletic directors, and teachers constantly ask themselves how they can best protect student athletes from injury and the school from liability.

Avoiding Negligence

As stated earlier in this text, most lawsuits alleging negligence begin in the classroom since that is where students spend most of their time. Other areas, however, are potentially more dangerous than the classroom; hence, educators will be expected to exhibit a higher standard. School athletic programs are clearly activities that are more dangerous than normal classroom activities.

Negligence is often alleged when a student is injured during a practice or game. Although the following discussion may appear to simply repeat material presented in the chapter on negligence, it is important to review the information in the special circumstances which athletic programs present. Negligence is an unintentional act or omission that results in injury. Persons who bring successful negligence suits are usually awarded financial damages in an amount calculated to compensate for the actual injury suffered. Punitive or exemplary damages can also be awarded. In assessing whether a person's behavior is negligent, a court will use the "reasonable person" test and question whether a reasonable person in the defendant's situation would have acted in this manner. "Reasonable" is whatever the jury or other factfinder decide. Before a court will find a defendant legally negligent, four elements, as previously discussed, must be present: *duty, violation of duty, proximate cause,* and *injury.* An examination of each of the four elements as applied to athletics should prove helpful to persons supervising athletic programs.

The Duty to Supervise

The individual charged with negligence must have a duty in the situation. Student athletes have a right to safety and coaches and other officials have a responsibility to protect the well being of all those entrusted to their care. Coaches have a duty to provide reasonable supervision of their players. Courts expect principals and athletic directors to develop, promulgate and implement rules and regulations that guide coaches in providing for student safety. Coaches should develop and implement further team practices that are consistent with safety and in harmony with administrative practices.

Violation of Duty

Negligence cannot exist if the second element, violation of duty, is not present. Courts understand that accidents and spontaneous actions can occur. The 1989 New York case, *Benitez v. NYC Board of Education,* involved a high school football player who was injured during play. The player alleged negligence on the part of the coach and principal for allowing him to play in a fatigued condition.

A lower court awarded the student damages, but the appellate court ruled that school officials had to provide only reasonable, not extraordinary, care and reversed the decision. Further, the court invoked the doctrine of assumption of the risk. Students are under no compulsion to play sports; if they choose to participate, they voluntarily assume the risks of some injuries. *Assumption of the risk* is a defense against an allegation of negligence.

At first glance, it may appear that athletic directors and coaches are the school officials who would be found liable for violation of duty in the case of student injury. Under the doctrine of *respondent superior,* let the superior answer, however, principals and administrators can be found liable for the acts of subordinates. For example, if a principal paid little or no attention to the administration of the athletic program, provided no supervision, and/or offered no guidance, he or she might be found liable for negligence if a student were injured while a dangerous practice or policy was in place. Unfortunately, many administrators believe themselves to be woefully ignorant of the principles of athletics and are too often content to let coaches and athletic directors run the sports program unsupervised. These same administrators would be shocked if someone were to suggest that a second year English teacher is an expert, needs no supervision, and should be given carte blanche in directing his classes.

Principals have an obligation to oversee athletics, while teachers must support the regulation of the athletic program. Certainly no one expects a principal to be an athletic expert, but the principal should be sure that only qualified individuals are hired as coaches and athletic directors. The principal should insist that the athletic director and/or coaches keep the administrator and teachers informed about the operation of the program.

Principals will not be held responsible for every mistake of employees but only for those that a reasonable person could have foreseen. Therefore, every principal and athletic director should have an athletic handbook outlining the policies and procedures for each sport. Parents and students should sign a statement agreeing to be governed by the provisions of the handbook

Proximate Cause

The third requirement for a finding of legal negligence is *proximate cause*. The violation of duty must be the proximate cause of the injury. Proximate cause is sometimes defined as contributing factor. If a coach were to order a 250-pound student to wrestle a 125-pound student and the lighter student were injured in the match, the coach is the proximate cause of the injury even though the physical actions of the heavier student are the direct cause of the injury.

The court must decide whether proper performance of duty could have prevented the injury and, in so doing, the court has to look at the facts of each individual case. In an old, but still applicable 1970 case, *Stehn v. MacFadden Foundations*, the Circuit Court of Appeals, Sixth Circuit, found a private school and its officials liable for damages sustained by a student who suffered a severe spinal cord injury in a wrestling match. The court found that the maneuver, which resulted in the injury, was not listed in any reputable book on the subject of teaching wrestling, and the defense could produce no evidence that the maneuver was legitimate. The coach had very limited previous experience and was coaching without any supervision.

The court ruled that the school's violation of duty—the failure to ensure that the coach was qualified and experienced—was the proximate cause of the student's injury. Proximate cause is a complex doctrine. It is difficult to predict what a court will determine to be the proximate cause in any particular allegation of negligence.

Injury

The fourth element necessary for a finding of negligence is injury. To prevail in a lawsuit, a student must have sustained an injury for which the court can award a remedy. No matter how unreasonable the behavior of a coach, there is no legal negligence if there is no injury. Everyone must understand, however, that physical harm is not the only type of injury; emotional or psychological harm can also constitute injury.

Grades and Exclusion from Athletics

Educators often face the problem of students who just barely miss attaining the necessary minimum grades to continue participation in a sport. Students, parents, and others can exert considerable pressure on teachers to change grades so that students can qualify to play. One might argue that such a practice is hardly the material of which lawsuits are made. Yet, anyone willing to pay a filing fee, can file a lawsuit against someone else. The suit may be without merit and eventually dismissed, but it will cause inconvenience. Even if no lawsuit is ever filed, there are issues of fairness.

One should note that problems result when minimum standards are not enforced or are arbitrarily lowered. If there is a rule requiring certain conduct or academic standards, educators should honor it. The rule should be adopted as school policy and exceptions should be avoided.

There is no absolute protection against lawsuits, particularly in athletics. Nonetheless, a thorough handbook, as indicated earlier, can provide the best possible protection and can serve as evidence that both parents and students understand the risks involved in sports and the requirements of participation in the school athletic program.

FOR REFLECTION AND DISCUSSION

- If asked, how would you describe the role of athletics in your school? What legal and ethical responsibilities do teachers have in regard to athletics?
- Student M, the star volleyball player, has asked you to give her one extra point on her grade so that she won't be suspended from the team and miss tournament play. She has offered to do extra work. Without M, there is very little chance that the team can win any of the tournament games. The coach has come to you on M's behalf, and you have a phone message that M's father, the chief justice of the state supreme court, has asked for a meeting with you. You must have a decision by 8:00 AM tomorrow. What will you do?

Chapter Fifteen

COPYRIGHT LAW, TECHNOLOGY AND CYBERSPACE

MOST EDUCATORS REALIZE that copyright law exists. If asked, many would probably respond that there are rules that should be followed when making copies of articles, book chapters, computer programs, DVDs, and television programs. For some individuals, the fact that apprehension and prosecution for breaking the copyright law rarely become reality makes them more willing to break the law. For others, their motive of helping students to learn is an excuse for failing to comply with the law.

Reasons to Copy

In the 1960s and 1970s budgetary considerations were the reasons given by churches, including Catholic churches, which copied songs from copyrighted works and used the copies to compile parish hymnals. Courts have consistently struck down such uses and have ordered the offending churches to pay damages.

Today, parishes and schools appear to be aware of the legal consequences of copying and many subscribe to the licensing arrangements of music companies. For a given sum of money, the institution can make as many copies of music as desired during the span of the contract.

However, it is not uncommon to find teachers copying such items as whole workbooks, other consumable materials, large portions of books and print materials. The swift advance of technology has catapulted computer programs, videocassettes and similar media into the sphere of teacher copying.

This chapter discusses copyright law as it applies to educational institutions, examines the tests of "fair use," and offers some guidelines for secondary school principals and teachers.

Copyright Law

Upon reflection, most educators would agree that copyright protection is a just law. Both the Copyright Act of 1909 (the Old Law) and the Copyright Act of 1976 (the New Law) represent attempts to safeguard the rights of authors. Persons who create materials are entitled to the fruits of their labors; those who use author's creations without paying royalties, buying copies or seeking permission are guilty of stealing.

It is tempting to think that copyright infringements and lawsuits are more or less the exclusive domain of large institutions. Certainly, the public learns about large-scale abuses faster than individual abuses. If a company is going to sue someone, it will seek a person or institution that has been guilty of multiple infringements so that larger damages can be won. It does not make good economic sense to sue someone who will be ordered to pay only a small amount of damages.

Sometimes, though, lawsuits are brought solely to prove a point. In 1983 case, *Marcus v. Rowley*, involving a dispute between two teachers in the same school, resulted in a federal court's ruling against the "copier." One teacher had prepared and copyrighted a 20-page booklet on cake decorating; the second teacher copied approximately half the pages and included them in her own materials. The amount of money involved was negligible; the author had sold fewer than 100 copies at a price of $2. Nonetheless, the court found the second teacher guilty of copyright violation; her use of the other's materials was not "fair."

What is Fair Use?

Section 107 of the 1976 Copyright Act states that fair use of copies in teaching is not an infringement of copyright. The sticking point is what the term "fair use" means. The section lists four factors to be included in any determination of fair use:

- The purpose and character of the use: Why is the copying being done?
- The nature of the copyrighted work: What is being copied? One page of a 150-page book? An entire poem?
- The amount and substantiality: What is copied—all of it? Some of it?
- The effect of the use on the copyright holder: Will the copying hurt sales?

Educators should have little or no trouble complying with the "purpose and character of the work" factor. Teachers generally copy materials to aid the educational process.

The Copyright Act of 1976 notes that "the nature of the copyrighted work" factor can prove more problematic than "character and purpose of the work." Who determines what is the nature of the work-the creator and/or copyright holder, the teacher, the judge and/or the jury? Almost any material can be classified as educational in some context; even a cartoon can be found to have some educational purpose if one is willing to look for it. It seems reasonable that, in determining nature, a court would look to the ordinary use of the work and to the author's intent in creating the work.

The "amount and substantiality" of the work copied is especially troublesome. Teachers understand that they are not supposed to copy a whole book, but may not understand that copying a television program or a movie onto a DVD or copying a computer program for student use can violate the "amount and substantiality" factor.

In the 1982 case of *Encyclopedia Britannica v. Crooks*, an educational company engaged in copying commercially available tapes and television programs for teachers, was found to be in violation of the Copyright Act. The company argued that it was providing an educational service for students and teachers who would otherwise be deprived of important educational opportunities. The U.S. District Court for the Western District of New York rejected the argument.

Teachers may be tempted to think that their small-scale copying acts could not compare with the scope of the activities in this case. In the majority of instances involving single copying, there is no comparison. One practice, developing libraries of copies, is not legally permissible. Whether the collections are of print materials or non-print materials, the practice of building collections can easily be subjected to the same scrutiny as the *Encyclopedia* case.

Would it be legally permissible if a campus ministry team recorded on a CD all the songs played on the retreat and then copied the CD for each retreat participant? The answer is "no." The only way such an action could be lawfully taken would be to obtain written permission from all the copyright holders to do so, an occurrence that would take time and would, in all likelihood, be unsuccessful.

It would also be illegal for the campus ministry team to allow the retreatants to download the CD into a portable music player such as an iPod or an MP3 device. While the retreatants might not view "downloaded music" as a violation of copyright laws, downloaded content, such as music and books, is protected by law.

The same copyright law also protects computer software. A parish or school may make one copy of a legally owned software program. This may be made for security purposes, as in the case of fire or other disaster. No other copies are permitted. The software industry works to identify illegal copies and aggressively pursues offenders. The fines for possession and use of illegal software can be much more than a parish or school can afford, in part because software companies desire to make a point about "pirated" intellectual property. The courts have been supportive of the companies, and cases are increasing both in number and in amounts of money awarded. Parishes and schools should maintain vigilance over all computers, and make certain that all software on them is legally owned. An annual or semi-annual inventory of computer programs is a good idea, as is a program that will erase programs added to computers by unauthorized users. There are programs available that will, at a certain time, each day, erase anything added to a computer's hard drive if a security code is not entered.

If there is any doubt as to the ownership of software, the best course of action is to erase the program or contact the authors and purchase the program. If school administrators have any doubt about a software program's legality, the EULA (End Use License Agreement) will explain how to contact the software maker.

The last of the four factors, "effect on the market," is difficult to apply to an educational setting. Arguments can be advanced that students would not rent or purchase commercially available items, even if the copies weren't available. It appears, though, that use of an author's work without appropriate payment for the privilege is a form of economic harm. Good faith generally will not operate as an acceptable defense in educational copyright or infringement cases. The Court for the Southern District of New York stated in *Roy v. Columbia Broadcasting System*: "The federal copyright statute protects copyrighted works against mere copying, even when done in good faith and even when not done to obtain a competitive advantage over the owners of the copyright in the infringed works."

Guidelines

A congressional committee developed "Guidelines for Classroom Copying in Not-for-Profit Educational Institutions," printed in House Report 94- 1476. 94th Congress 2d Session (1976). Principals should ensure that teachers have access to copies of the guidelines, which are readily available from local libraries, the Copyright Office, and members of Congress. Although these guidelines do not have the force of law that the statute has, judges have used them in deciding cases. Some examples of the guidelines follow.

For poetry, copying of a complete poem of less than 250 words printed on no more than two pages or of an excerpt of 250 words from a longer poem is allowed. For prose, a complete work of less than 2,500 words or an excerpt from a longer work of not more than 1,000 words or 10% of the work is permissible. The guidelines mandate that copying meet this test of brevity.

The copying must be spontaneous. The teacher must have decided more or less on the spur of the moment to use an item. Spontaneity presumes that a teacher did not have time to secure permission for use from the copyright holder. A teacher who decides in September to use certain materials in December has ample time to seek permission. In such a situation, failure to seek permission means that the spontaneity requirement will not be met.

A last requirement is that the copying must not have a *cumulative effect*. Making copies of poems by one author would have a cumulative effect and would mean that collected works of the author would not be bought.

Videotapes, DVDs (Digital Video Discs), and movies or television broadcasts copied to a DVR (Digital Video Recorder such as TIVO) should be kept for no longer than 45 days. During the first 10 days, a teacher may use the tape once in a class (although there is a provision for one repetition for legitimate instructional review). For the remaining 35 days teachers may use the copied material for evaluative purposes only.

Moral, Ethical, and Legal-Challenges Relating to Technology

Thirty years ago, most educators had limited access to computer technology. Today, it is hard to imagine life without computers and the related technology of the Information Age. Access to volumes of information that would have taken much time to gather a few years ago can now be obtained in a few moments with the aid of a modem and a database. These developments present challenges for the educator who seeks to act in ways that are morally, ethically and legally correct.

Appropriateness of Available Materials

Headlines reveal that several young persons have run away from home as a result of propositions received from persons on the Internet. Since there currently is no truly effective means of monitoring and/or censoring material on the Internet and other networks, there is nothing to prevent unsupervised young people from being in electronic conversation with inappropriate persons about sexual matters, drugs, crime, and other less than suitable topics. The growing popularity of "chat rooms" presents a particular ethical/moral dilemma. Since there are no privacy police, people who log into a chat room can write anything they wish to another person "in the room" at the same time. E-mail provides a means for persons with no prior knowledge of each other to share intimate conversation.

"Chat rooms" and e-mail present issues of morality not unlike those presented by television and movies. The television industry polices itself, at least to a degree. For example, one does not generally find prime-time pornography on the major networks. Although adult channels are available on cable TV, parents and other supervisors can purchase devices that allow them to block access to such channels. Hotels and motels allow parents to call the front desk and have access to movie channels blocked in their rooms.

The movie industry provides a rating system that indicates the appropriateness of content for certain age groups. The dearth of G and PG movies, however, indicates that movies without sex and violence do not generally sell as well as those containing such elements.

With no equivalent monitoring system in place in the world of cyberspace, parents and other educators must maintain constant vigilance. The First Amendment to the Constitution does permit much leeway in terms of expression, but it does not require that children and teenagers be given unlimited access to other persons' self-expression. Adults must stand firm and monitor computer usage by the young people for whom they are responsible.

Principals are responsible for supervision of all aspects of the educational process. If a teacher is charged with copyright violation, it is likely that the principal will be charged as well. Clear policies and careful monitoring of those policies can lessen exposure to liability. As many legal authorities have observed, copyright violation is stealing.

Educators may be tempted to believe the oft-quoted lines from Shakespear's *The Merchant of Venice*, "To do a great right, do a little wrong" (IV, I, 215). Ethical, moral, and legal imperatives do not accept such rationalization. Students, rich or poor, have a right to experience the richness of technology. At the same time, they have a right to expect that adults will protect them from harm and will exercise vigilance over technological, as well as other, behaviors. Lastly, educators themselves must be models of integrity and observe the laws that grant authors and other creators the right to the fruits of their labors. Obviously, the Internet and the Information Highway were not part of Jesus' life experience, but it is appropriate to reflect on how He would want us to meet the challenges they present in today's world. Catholic educators must surely model their behavior on that of Jesus who scrupulously paid the temple tax, rendered Caesar his due, and exhorted landowners to pay workers a generous wage.

FOR REFLECTION AND DISCUSSION

- Six students have just told you that student A, who has managed to bypass the lockout, has been logging onto a chat-room and is planning to visit a 40 year old woman he met on the "May/December Romance Hotline." What will you do?
- You are planning a production of Oklahoma for March. The licensing fee is very high. A friend of yours has 20 copies of the librettos and scripts. He says the company didn't ask for them back. He offers to give them to you. How will you respond?
- The club you moderate decided to see t-shirts as a fundraiser. You had the flu the week the orders were due. The students, knowing you had approved the fundraiser, ordered the t-shirts. They have been delivered, and the excited students brought you one. Your heart sinks when you see the Peanuts' character, Snoopy, on the front of the shirt. You know that the owners of Charles Schultz's characters and comic strips do not allow free use of any of Schultz's work. The shirts are supposed to go on sale tomorrow. What will you do?

Chapter Sixteen

BLOGGING, DANGER AND EDUCATOR RESPONSIBILITY

ONE OF THE MORE RECENT ISSUES demanding educator attention is blogging. Not so long ago, many readers would not have recognized the term, which means the keeping of an on-line log or journal. The site, myspace.com and its progeny began innocently enough. Adults were able to share thoughts with other bloggers and site visitors. Some persons, unable to find publishers for articles, began to post them through blogs and eventually, sell subscriptions to their sites/works. Generally, more sophisticated than chat rooms in terms of conversational type and content, site providers, nonetheless, provided little or no monitoring of content or bloggers. Sites often include a statement that all bloggers must be at least 16 or 18 years of age; however, there is no way to ensure that persons under the minimum age will not have access.

Students generally blog from home, not school, but two problem areas cause administrative concern: (1) blogger safety and (2) the appropriateness of what the blogger posts.

Safety

Young school age bloggers often post identifying personal information that can have tragic consequences. Anyone with Internet access, including sexual predators and murderers, can log onto a blog. Many young people do not seem to understand mortality, at least their own. Bad things happen to "other people." However, nothing prevents a predator from noting a child or adolescent's picture, address, phone number, school, extra-curricular activities, and making plans to intercept the younger person. The author presents workshops and seminars on blogging and Internet safety to administrators, other educators and parents. Occasionally, she speaks to elementary and high school students. One group of high school students was attentive, polite and respectfully challenging. However, most of them could not "get" it—that posting pictures and personal information on blogs or other sites could prove fatal. "Come on, Sister," protested one attractive teenage girl, "Nothing like that would happen here. This isn't a big city; it's a small town." Students at Columbine High School probably held similar beliefs before tragedy occurred. No one's safety can be guaranteed. Educator responsibilities do not begin and end with the school day. Student safety must be paramount. Whatever can be done to protect students and educate parents should be done, regardless of whether the law requires it.

Student Discipline

Any seasoned administrator has probably had at least one parent or student argue, "It happened outside school/the school day. You can't punish me for what I did on my own time." The fact, however, is that a Catholic school or program administrator can impose consequences for conduct occurring outside school. What students do off-campus can detrimentally impact a school or program's reputation. So long as the parent/student handbook, which can and should be a contract, states that the administration reserves the right to discipline students for off-campus conduct, courts will not interfere. The school should require that prior to the student's first day of attendance, parents sign a statement that they agree to be bound by the handbook's rules and regulations. Courts will uphold rules and regulations that are not illegal.

Educators are already familiar with the issues arising from student threats conveyed through e-mail. Blogging provides another venue for making threats. Threats are threats wherever they are made. Individual blogs have been, and continue to be used, to plot crimes and to solicit criminal activity. If challenged, the blogger will generally claim that he or she was joking. If a crime occurs, especially if someone is injured or killed, who is responsible? The blogger who posts a solicitation such as, "I need someone to kill my brother. I will pay in money or sex," but claims after the fact to be joking or is the person who actually did the deed? Can both be held responsible?

A more common problem occurs when students make negative, often untruthful statements about staff and other students. In addition to blogging opportunities, some websites provide a place to "rate" teachers and to post potentially defamatory statements. Holding that teachers were, in effect, quasi-public figures and had to expect a certain amount of "grief" from parents and students, courts in the past were reluctant to find in favor of teachers who brought defamation suits against parents or students. Such is no longer the case. Several state courts have ruled that teachers and administrators have the same right to their reputations, as do other people. Therefore, if defamed, educators have a right to sue.

Additionally, school administrators can punish students who defame others in the school community. Deliberate defamation of others is not consistent with Christian values and students should be held accountable for intentional harm they cause others.

Use of School Name and Logo on Personal Blogs

The school or parish owns the school or program's name and administrators have the right to restrict its use. An administrator can determine that a Saturday trip to an amusement park organized by parents is not a school event and can decline to allow the use of the school name; in the same way, rules can prohibit unauthorized use of names and logos on blogs.

Teachers and Blogs

It is not uncommon for teachers to have blogs. Some individuals use blogs as a way to communicate with friends and families. However, virtually anyone can visit a blog, so teacher bloggers must be extremely careful in what they post. A blog is no place to announce and/or discuss frustration with one's school, boss, the curriculum, the students, the parents, etc. Some of the cautions suggested earlier in the text apply in cyberspace as well as in face-to-face interactions. Before posting anything on a blog or a website, a person should ask, "How would this look in the newspaper or on the evening news? Can someone read something into this that I did not intend? Could any of this be considered defamatory? How would I feel if someone else wrote this and I read it?" Perhaps the best question to ask is the one posed by the "mom" test: "What would my mother say if she saw it?" It is far better to refrain from posting something than to spend years regretting what was posted and perhaps never being able to rectify the damage.

For Reflection and Discussion

- You are class moderator. The class president tells you that the officers want to start a myspace page about the class. He says that only the officers will post information and will carefully monitor it to be sure that nothing inappropriate is posted. How will you respond?

- You were surfing the net recently and the blog of a student in the school appeared. The blog does not mention the school by name, but a picture posted on it was taken in front of the school and part of a sign with the school name is visible. In the blog, the student expresses support for a number of positions inconsistent with the teachings of the Catholic Church. She states that she is a member of several pro-choice groups, has participated in pro-choice rallies and has had two abortions herself, even though she is a student in a Catholic school. A second section is devoted to a justification of euthanizing the elderly and the weak. You could, of course, never mention that you saw it. You could confront the student. You could report the student and her blog to the school administration. What would you do and why?

GLOSSARY OF LEGAL TERMS

Common Law

Common law is that law not created by a legislature. It includes principles of action based on long-established standards of reasonable conduct and on court judgments affirming such standards. It is sometime called "judge-made law."

Compelling State Interest

Compelling state interest is the overwhelming or serious need for governmental action. The government is said to have a compelling state interest in anti-discrimination legislation and in the elimination of unequal treatment of citizens.

Contract

A contract is an agreement between two parties. The essentials of a contract are: (1) mutual assent (2) by legally competent parties (3) for consideration (4) to subject matter that is legal and (5) in a form of agreement that is legal.

Defamation

Defamation is an unprivileged communication. It can be either spoken (slander) or written (libel).

Due Process (constitutional)

Due process is fundamental fairness under the law. There are two types:
Substantive Due Process: The constitutional guarantee that no person shall be arbitrarily deprived of his life, liberty, or property; the essence of substantive due process is protection from arbitrary unreasonable action" (Black). Substantive due process concerns what is done as distinguished from *how* it is done (procedural due process).

Procedural Due Process: how the process of depriving someone of something is carried out; *how it is done.* The minimum requirements of constitutional due process are *notice* and a *hearing* before an *impartial tribunal.*

Foreseeability

Foreseeability is the "the reasonable anticipation that harm or injury is the likely result of acts or omission" (Black). It is not necessary that a person anticipate the particular injury that might result from an action, but only that danger or harm in general might result.

Negligence

Negligence is the absence of the degree of care, which a reasonable person would be expected to use in a given situation. Legal negligence requires the presence of four elements: duty, violation of duty, proximate cause, and injury.

Policy

A policy is a guide for discretionary action. Policy states what is to be done, not how it is to be done.

Proximate Cause

Proximate cause is a contributing factor to an injury. The injury was the result of or reasonably foreseeable outcome of the action or inaction said to be the proximate cause.

State Action

State action is the presence of the government in an activity to such a degree that the activity may be considered to be that of the government.

Tort

A tort is a civil or private wrong as distinguished from a crime.

WORKS CITED

Americans with Disabilities Act of 1990.

Benitez v. NYC B.O.E. 543, N.Y.2d 29 (1989).

Brooks v. Logan and Joint District No. 2 127 of Idaho 484, 903 p. 2d. 73 (1995).

The Buckley Amendment of 1975 and the Family Educational Rights and Privacy Act 34 CFR Part 99, 1975.

Civil Rights Act of 1964, Pub. 88-352, 78 Sqt. 241, 1964.

Code of Canon Law of 1983, prepared by Canon Law Society of America, Washington, D.C.

Copyright Act of 1909.

Copyright Act of 1976, U.S. Code 17, Title 17.

Jane Doe v. Spec. Sch. Dis. of St. Louis County, 901 F.2d 642 (8th Cir. 1990).

D.T. et al v. Ind. Sch. Dis. No. 16 of Pawnee City, 894 F.2d 11 76 (1980).

Encyclopedia Brittanica v. Crooks, 542 F. Supp. 11 56 (W.D.N.Y. 1982).

Franklin v. Gwinnet County Public Schools 503 U.S. 60 (1992).

Garner, Bryan A. (ed.) (1999). Black's Law Dictionary (7th ed.) St. Paul: West.

Geraci v. St. Xavier High School, 12 Ohio Op. 3d 146 (Ohio, 1978).

"Guidelines for Classroom Copying in Not-for-Profit Educational Institutions", House Report 94- 1476, 94Ih Congress 2d Session (1976).

Individuals with Disabilities in Education Act (IDEA)Amendments (1997).

Levandoski b. Jackson City School District, 328 So. 2d 339 Minnesota (1976)

Marcus v. Rowley, 695 F.2d 11 71 (1983).

Medlin v. Bass, 327 N.C. 587, 398 S.E. 2d 460 (1990).

New Jersey v. T.L.O., 105 S. Ct. 733 (1985).

No Child Left Behind Act of 2001, P.L. 107-110.

Pastoral Statement of U.S. Catholic Bishops on Handicapped People (1978).

Rehabilitation Act of 1973, Section 504, P.L. 93 -112 93rd Congress, H.R. 8070.

Rendell-Baker v. Kohn, 102 S.Ct. 2764 (1982).

Roy v. Columbia Broadcasting System, 503 F.Supp. 1137 (S.D.N.Y. 1980).

Shakespeare, William. The Merchant of Venice.

Smith v. Archbishop of St. Louis, 632 S.W.2d 51 6 (I982).

Stehn v. MacFadden Foundations, 434 F.2d 811 (U.S.C.A. 6th Cir., 1970).

Tinker v. Des Moines Independent Community School District et al., 393 U.S. 503 (1969).

ABOUT THE AUTHOR

Sister Mary Angela Shaughnessy, SCN

SISTER MARY ANGELA SHAUGHNESSY, a sister of Charity of Nazareth, holds a Bachelor's degree in English, a Masters degree in English, a Masters and Ph.D. in Educational Administration, and a Juris Doctorate in Law. Her research centers on the law as it affects Catholic education and Church ministry. She is the author of over thirty texts.

Sr. Shaughnessy has taught at all levels of education. For eight years she was a high school principal, for twenty-one years she served as professor emerita of education at Spalding University, and has served as an adjunct professor in various college and university programs. Sr. Shaughnessy is general counsel and executive director of the Education Law Institute sponsored at St. Catharine College in Springfield, Kentucky. She has received numerous awards including the Michael J. Guerra Leadership Award at the NCEA Convention in 2008. In 1997, she was named one of the twenty-five most influential persons in Catholic education.

Texts by Mary Angela Shaughnessy, SCN
Available for Purchase from NCEA

2007   Compendium of Articles on Legal Issues: 1990-2010.

2007   Volunteers in Catholic Schools: Legal Issues.

2006   Legal Issues for the Catechetical Leader.
        Legal Issues for the Catechist, Youth Minister and Teacher.

2005   Legal Issues for Coaches and Moderators in Catholic Schools:
        A Handbook.
        The Law and Catholic Schools: Legal Issues for the Third
        The Millennium

2004   Policy Formation in Catholic Education.

2003   Campus Ministry and the Law.
        Home and School Working Together: The Rights and Re-
        sponsibilities of Catholic School Parents (pamphlet, 2nd ed.)

2002   School Handbooks: Legal Considerations. (2nd ed.).

2001   A Primer on Law for Administrators and Boards, Commis-
        sions and Councils of Catholic Education.

1998   Selected Legal Issues in Catholic Schools (1st ed.)

1996   Religious Education and the Law: A Handbook for Catechet-
        ical Religious Education and the Law: A Catechist Hand-
        book.

1995   Home and School Working Together: Catholic School Par-
        ents'
        Rights and Responsibilities. (1st ed.)

1993   Ethics and the Law: A Teacher's Guide to Decision-Making.
        (with John Shaughnessy) .

1993   Volunteers in Catholic Schools: An Administrator's Guide to
        Legal Considerations. (with John Shaughnessy and Maureen
        Coughlin).

1992   A Primer on Law for DREs and Youth Ministers.
        Washington, D.C.: NCEA. ISBN 1-55833-113-1.

1991   Extended Care Programs in Catholic Schools: Some Legal
        Considerations. (1st ed.)

1990   Catholic Pre-Schools: Some Legal Concerns. (1st ed.)

1989   School Handbooks: Legal Considerations. (1st ed.)

1988   A Primer on School Law: A Guide for Board Members in
        Catholic Schools. (1st ed.